PARAMORE

Books LLC®, Wiki Series, Memphis, USA, 2011. ISBN: 9781156958186. www.booksllc.net
Copyright: http://creativecommons.org/licenses/by-sa/3.0/deed.en

Table of Contents

Paramore
List of awards and nominations received by Paramore............................. 1
Paramore 1
Paramore's Videos. All of Them. Ever... 6

Paramore albums
2010 Summer Tour EP........................ 7
All We Know Is Falling..................... 7
Brand New Eyes 0
Live in the UK 2008 7
Paramore discography........................ 8
Riot! 8
The Final Riot! 9

The Summer Tic EP 10

Paramore concert tours
Brand New Eyes World Tour............. 10
Honda Civic Tour............................... 12
Summer Tour 2009 (No Doubt)........ 13

Paramore members
Hayley Williams 14
Jeremy Davis 14
Josh Farro... 15
Taylor York 16
Zac Farro 16

Paramore songs

All We Know 17
Brick by Boring Brick....................... 17
Careful (Paramore song) 18
Crushcrushcrush................................. 18
Decode (song) 19
Emergency (song) 20
Hallelujah (Paramore song)............... 20
Ignorance (song)................................ 20
List of Paramore songs..................... 22
Misery Business 22
Playing God (song) 23
Pressure (Paramore song).................. 24
That's What You Get 24
The Only Exception 25

Introduction

Purchase of this book entitles you to a free trial membership in the publisher's book club at www.booksllc.net. (Time limited offer.) Simply enter the barcode number from the back cover onto the membership form. The book club entitles you to select from hundreds of thousands of books at no additional charge. You can also download a digital copy of this and related books to read on the go. Simply enter the title or subject onto the search form to find them.

Each chapter in this book ends with a URL to a hyperlinked online version. Type the URL exactly as it appears. If you change the URL's capitalization it won't work. Use the online version to access related pages, websites, footnotes, tables, color photos, updates. Click the version history tab to see the chapter's contributors. Click the edit link to suggest changes.

A large and diverse editor base collaboratively wrote the book, not a single author. After a long process of discussion and debate, the chapters gradually took on a neutral point of view reached through consensus. Additional editors expanded and contributed to chapters striving to achieve balance and comprehensive coverage. This reduced the regional or cultural bias found in many other books and provided access and breadth on subject matter otherwise little documented.

List of awards and nominations received by Paramore

Paramore is an American band from Franklin, Tennessee.

Source (edited): "http://en.wikipedia.org/wiki/List_of_awards_and_nominations_received_by_Paramore"

Paramore

Paramore is an American rock band from Franklin, Tennessee, formed in 2004. The band consists of lead vocalist Hayley Williams, bassist Jeremy Davis, and guitarist Taylor York. The group released its debut album *All We Know Is Falling* in 2005, and its second album *Riot!* in 2007, which was certified Platinum in the US and Gold in Australia, Canada, New Zealand, and the UK. *Brand New Eyes*, Paramore's third album, was released in 2009 and is the band's highest charting album to date.

History

2002–2004: Formation

In 2002, at age 13, vocalist Hayley Williams moved from her hometown Meridian, Mississippi to Franklin, Tennessee where she met brothers Josh Farro and Zac Farro while she was attending a private school. Shortly after arriving, she began taking vocal lessons with Brett Manning. Prior to forming Paramore, Williams and bassist Jeremy Davis, along with friend Kimee Read, took part in a funk cover band called The Factory, while Josh and Zac Farro had practiced together after school. The other members of what was soon to be Paramore had been "edgy about the whole female thing" of having Williams as vocalist, but, because they were really good friends, she started writing for them. Williams said of the guys when she first met them, "They were the first people I met who were as passionate about music as I was." The band was officially formed by Josh Farro (lead guitar/backing vocals), Zac Farro (drums), Jeremy Davis (bass guitar) and Hayley Williams (lead vocals) in 2004, with the later addition of Williams' neighbor Jason Bynum (rhythm guitar). When Davis showed up, he was stunned to find out the drummer was only twelve years old. He admitted "I had very, very, very, little faith in everyone in the band because of their age. I remember thinking, 'This is not going to work because this kid is way too young,' but that first day of practice was amazing. I knew we were on to something." According to Williams, the name "Paramore" came from the maiden name of the mother of one of their first bass players. Once the group learned the meaning of the homophone "paramour" ("secret lover"), they decided to adopt the name, using the *Paramore* spelling.

Williams was originally signed to Atlantic Records as a solo artist in 2003. She had been introduced to Atlantic A&R Tom Storms through Kent Marcus and Jim Zumwalt, lawyers of managers Dave Steunebrink and Richard Williams, and then eventually signed to Atlantic by Jason Flom. Steunebrink and Richard Williams had originally discovered and signed her to a production deal that was later bought out by Atlantic. The original plan of the label was to turn her into a pop singer, but Williams resisted, saying that she wanted to play alternative rock music and wanted a band behind her. In an interview with HitQuarters the band's A&R at Atlantic, Steve Robertson, said, "She wanted to make sure that we didn't look at her as some straight to Top 40 pop princess. She wanted to make sure that she and her band got the chance to show what they can do as a rock band writing their own songs." Label president Julie Greenwald and the label staff decided to go with her wishes. The original management team for the band was Dave Steunebrink, Creed manager Jeff Hanson, and Hanson's assistant Mark Mercado.

Paramore were originally supposed to come out on Atlantic Records but the label's marketing department decided it would be better for the image of the band to not have them attached to a major label. They instead released their music through a cooler niche label in Fueled by Ramen. Head of Warner Music Group, Lyor Cohen had already identified Fueled by Ramen as a label they should partner with and it was decided the rock label would make an ideal match for Paramore. According to Robertson, when the band were presented to Fueled by Ramen's CEO John Janick, "he got the vision of the band immediately." Janick went to a Taste of Chaos performance in Orlando, Florida to see the band perform live. In April 2005, after a smaller private performance at a warehouse, the band was signed to Atlantic Records and Fueled By Ramen.

The band's first song written together was "Conspiracy", which was later used on their debut album. In 2004, they were a featured band in Purple Door. At this time, they were touring the southeast, usually being driven by Williams' parents. She commented that "Back then, I guess we were all thinking, after school we'll go to the house and practice. It was what we loved to do for fun, and still do! I don't think any of us really knew this would turn out to be what it's become."

2005–2006: *All We Know Is Falling*

Paramore traveled back to Orlando, Florida, but shortly after arriving, Jeremy Davis left the band, citing personal reasons. The remaining four members of Paramore continued with the album, writing "All We Know" about his departure, and later deciding to base *All We Know Is Falling* around the concept. The album artwork also reflected Paramore's grief as Hayley Williams explains, "The couch on the cover of *All We Know is Falling* with no one there and the shadow walking away; it's all about Jeremy leaving us and us feeling like there's an empty space." Recording took three weeks, and promotional material for the album only featured the four remaining members.

Before touring, the band added John Hembree (bass guitar) to their line up to replace Jeremy Davis. During that summer, Paramore was featured on the Shira Girl stage of the 2005 Warped Tour. After being asked by the band, Jeremy Davis returned to Paramore after five months apart, replacing Hembree. *All We Know Is Falling* was released on July 24, 2005, and reached #30 on the Billboard's Heatseekers Chart. Paramore released "Pressure" as its first single, with a video directed by Shane Drake, but the song had failed to place in the charts. The video featured the band performing in a warehouse, eventually getting sprayed with water sprinklers as the storyline of a conflicted couple occurs. In July, "Emergency" was released as the second single, the video again reuniting the band with director Shane Drake and featuring Hunter Lamb (rhythm guitar), who replaced Jason Bynum. The video for "Emergency" showcased Paramore in another performance, this time fixing the members bloody costumes. The third single, "All We Know", was released with limited airtime, with the video consisting of a collection of live performances and backstage footage.

In January 2006, the band took part in the Winter Go West tour where they played alongside Seattle bands Amber Pacific and The Lashes. In February, Hayley Williams was featured on "Keep Dreaming Upside Down" by October Fall. In spring of 2006, Paramore was an opening act on headlining tours for both Bayside and soon afterwards, The

Rocket Summer. They toured the United Kingdom from October 5 to October 15, 2006, where they ended in London at The Mean Fiddler. The band then covered Foo Fighters' "My Hero" for the *Sound of Superman* soundtrack which was released on June 26, 2006.

During the summer of 2006, Paramore played a portion of Warped Tour, primarily on the Volcom and Hurley Stages, and their first night on the Main Stage was at a date in their hometown of Nashville. Paramore's first United States headlining tour began on August 2, 2006 to a sold-out audience with support from This Providence, Cute Is What We Aim For, and Hit the Lights with the final show in Nashville. That year they were voted "Best New Band", and Hayley Williams was voted as #2 "Sexiest Female", by readers of the British magazine *Kerrang!*.

In 2007, Hunter Lamb left the group to get married, and Paramore continued onward as a quartet. Paramore was then named by British magazine *NME* as one of ten bands to watch out for in their "New Noise 2007" feature. In January, the band played an acoustic set for the grand opening of a Warped Tour exhibit at the Rock and Roll Hall of Fame, and the dress Hayley Williams wore in the video for "Emergency" was also put on display in the exhibit.

Paramore was featured in *Kerrang!* magazine once more, however, Hayley Williams believed the article was an untrue portrayal of the band, particularly because it focused on her as the main component. Afterwards, Williams addressed the issue in the band's LiveJournal, with a post saying, "we could've done without a cover piece. sorry, if it offends anyone at Kerrang! but i don't think there was one bit of truth in that article." In April, Hayley Williams' vocals were featured in "Then Came To Kill" by The Chariot. They headlined a tour in early 2007 with This Providence, The Almost and Love Arcade.

2007–2008: *Riot!* and other projects

Lead vocalist Hayley Williams (left) and rhythm guitarist Taylor York (right) perform at the Vans Warped Tour in Vancouver, July 2007

Paramore began recording their second album, *Riot!* in January 2007, ending production in March without rhythm guitarist Hunter Lamb (who left the band early in 2007 after getting married); without Lamb, lead guitarist Josh Farro was required to play both guitar parts on the album. Taylor York, who had been in a band with the Farro brothers before the two met Hayley Williams, joined as a replacement for Lamb. After being courted by producers Neal Avron and Howard Benson, Paramore opted to record *Riot!* with New Jersey producer David Bendeth (Your Vegas, Breaking Benjamin), releasing the album on June 12, 2007. *Riot!* entered the Billboard 200 at number 20, the UK charts at number 24, and sold 44,000 its first week in the United States.

The name *Riot!* had been chosen because it meant "a sudden outburst of uncontrolled emotion", and it was a word that "summed it all up". The first single from the album, released June 21, 2007, "Misery Business", is, according to Williams, "more honest than anything I've ever written, and the guys matched that emotion musically."

Summer of 2007 saw Paramore participating on their third Warped Tour and posting journals of their experiences on yourhereblog for MTV. In June they were declared by Rolling Stone as "Ones to Watch". Paramore made their live television debut on Fuse Networks daily show, The Sauce. The second single from *Riot!*, "Hallelujah", was released on July 30, 2007, and is only available online and on UK television. The video, much like "All We Know", features backstage footage and live performances.

In August 2007, Paramore had been featured in television spots on MTV, performing acoustic versions of their songs or acting in short accompaniments to MTV program commercials. As "MTV Artists of the Week", the band filmed the faux camping themed spots in Queens, New York, all written and directed by Evan Silver and Gina Fortunato. MTV.com also has a collection of short videos with the band to promote *Riot!* as well. For weeks in August 2007, the "Misery Business" video was the number one streamed video at MTV.com. On October 8, Paramore played "Misery Business" live on *Late Night with Conan O'Brien*, a booking made possible due to the friendship struck between the band and Max Weinberg during the 2007 Warped Tour. In August, Paramore participated in New Found Glory's music video for their cover of Sixpence None the Richer's song "Kiss Me".

On October 11, 2007, the music video for "Crushcrushcrush" debuted on the United States television as the next single from *Riot!*. The video for "Crushcrushcrush" featured the band playing a performance in a barren desert, being spied upon, and later destroying their equipment. The single was released in the United States on November 19 and made available in the United Kingdom on November 12, 2007. Hayley Williams recorded guest vocals for the tracks "The Church Channel" and "Plea" for the Say Anything concept album *In Defense of the Genre* released on October 23, 2007. The group performed live, acoustic style in Boston on November 29, 2007 for FNX radio. On December 31, 2007, Paramore performed on the MTV New Year's Eve program which ran from 11:30 p.m. to 1:00 a.m.

Paramore at *The Social*, Orlando, Florida on April 23, 2007.

Paramore was featured on the cover of February 2008 issue of *Alternative Press* magazine and voted "Best Band Of 2007" by the readers. The band was nominated for "Best New Artist" at the 50th Annual Grammy Awards presented on February 10, 2008 but lost to Amy Winehouse. Early 2008 saw Paramore touring the United Kingdom, supporting their album *Riot!*, along with New Found Glory, Kids in Glass Houses and Conditions. In early February 2008, the band began a tour in Europe, however on February 21, 2008, the band announced that they had canceled six shows due to personal issues. Williams wrote on the band's web site that "the break will give that band 'a chance to get away and work out our personal issues'". MTV.com reported that fans of Paramore were speculating about the future of the band and reported rumors of trouble had begun earlier in the month when Josh Farro expressed his anger against the media's focus on Hayley Williams. The band, however, returned to their hometown to record the music video for the fourth single "That's What You Get", which was then released on March 24, 2008.

The band toured with Jimmy Eat World in the United States in April and May 2008. The band headlined the Give It A Name festival in the United Kingdom on May 10 and May 11, 2008. Also the band performed on the In New Music We Trust Stage at Radio 1's One Big Weekend in Mote Park, Kent on May 10, 2008. Paramore played their first Ireland show at the RDS in Dublin on June 2, 2008, followed by the 2008 Vans Warped Tour from July 1–6.

On MTV's *TRL*, May 7, 2008, lead singer Hayley Williams said that the band was working on a new album and that it would hopefully be released by next summer. Hayley Williams says she and the band have been practicing the new songs during the sound checks on tour. In an *Alternative Press* cover story, Zac Farro speculated on a forthcoming album, saying that it would sound like bands Mew, Thrice, and Arcade Fire.

On May 19, 2008, Paramore announced on their website that they will be going on tour again, the tour being named "The Final Riot!", starting July 25 and ending September 1. On this tour, the band performed part of Leonard Cohen's "Hallelujah". On September 2, 2008, Paramore released a collaboration hoodie along with Hurley Clothing based on the album *Riot!*. All proceeds went to the Love146 foundation.

Paramore's song "Decode" was the lead single for the novel-based *Twilight* film. Another song called "I Caught Myself" is also featured on the film's soundtrack. "Decode" was released on October 1, 2008 on the Paramore Fan Club site as well as Stephenie Meyer's website. The band began shooting the video October 13 and it premiered on November 3. Hot Topic hosted listening parties for the soundtrack on October 24, 2008, and the album was released on November 4, 2008. Borders released an exclusive version of the soundtrack that features an acoustic version of "Decode."

The band released a live album named *The Final Riot!* on November 25, 2008. The album includes a bonus DVD with a full concert recorded in Chicago, as well as a behind the scenes documentary. As of the 9 of April 2009, *The Final Riot!* is certified gold in the United States.

2009–2010: *Brand New Eyes* and touring

In January 2009, Josh Farro spoke about the band's upcoming third studio album. Talking to *Kerrang!*, Farro said: "We're gonna try to [record] it in Nashville. I think writing the album there will inspire us, and then if we record there too it'll be a lot easier since we can sleep in our beds at night rather than in hotels like the other 300 days out of the year! We're not sure who's going to produce the record yet. We did "Decode" with [producer] Rob Cavallo, which was a good experience, but we're looking around and don't want to make any decisions until we have a lot of songs and we know what we're looking for. We really enjoy our live sound and we want a producer who can really capture that."

Paramore in the tour Brand New Eyes World Tour at the Warfield in US

On January 21, 2009, it was announced that Paramore will be the special guest with Bedouin Soundclash, The Sounds and Janelle Monae at the No Doubt Summer Tour 2009, starting in May 2009 in outdoor amphitheaters and arenas across the US and Canada.

Paramore wrote and completed their newest record *Brand New Eyes* in early 2009. The first single off of the album was "Ignorance" and was released July 7, 2009. The official music video for "Ignorance" aired on all MTV platforms, networks, and websites on August 13, 2009. Paramore, along with Paper Route and The Swellers, toured in support of *Brand New Eyes* in the fall of 2009. Some tour dates were postponed due to Hayley Williams becoming infected with laryngitis. "Brick By Boring Brick", "The Only Exception", "Careful" and "Playing God" followed as the album's next singles. To promote the album, the band recorded a performance for *MTV Unplugged*.

Paramore then played a sold out 15-date European tour with You Me At Six, Paper Route and Now Now Every Children. Their stadium tour culminated at London's Wembley Arena, to an audience of 12,500. The band performed in 2010 in the Australian Soundwave Festival along with bands such as Faith No More, Placebo, You Me at Six, All Time Low, Jimmy Eat World and Taking Back Sunday. Shortly before the tour, lead guitarist Josh Farro announced via the band's LiveJournal that he is engaged and stayed behind to plan his wedding. Justin York, brother of Taylor York, filled in for him on the tour. The band, with Farro returned, embarked on a spring tour of the U.S. in late April. Paramore supported Green Day on selected dates of their Stadium tour, in Dublin and Paris.

In April 2010, the band announced that they would be headlining the 2010 Honda Civic Tour. The tour began on July 23 in Raleigh, NC and closed on September 19 in Anaheim, CA. After a short United Kingdom tour in November 2010, the band announced, on December 2, 2010, the official dates for a South American tour to take place during February and March 2011.

During an interview with MTV at the Z100 Jingle Ball on December 11, 2010, Hayley and Taylor announced that the band would be taking a break after their South American Tour in 2011 to write for their forthcoming fourth studio album.

Josh Farro in Vancouver in the Summer Tour 2009

On December 18, 2010 a message from Hayley, Jeremy, and Taylor was released through Paramore.net stating that Josh and Zac were leaving the band. In the message they stated, "A couple of months ago, Josh and Zac let us know they would be leaving the band after our show in Orlando last Sunday. None of us were really shocked. For the last year it hasn't seemed as if they wanted to be around anymore. We want Josh and Zac to do something that makes them happy and if that isn't here with us, then we support them finding happiness elsewhere. But we never for a second thought about leaving any of this behind." The post also stated that the remaining members had no intention of disbanding. They also added "As we look back, and now as we look with excitement to the future, in all of this what truly matters are the good times. The pictures of us with our arms around each other, the long van rides, your faces while you sing along as we play. Thank you for getting us right here to this very moment. We look forward to our best times. And we hope you will go there with us." The band also confirmed the scheduled South American tour is still going to happen.

Josh Farro wrote a personal response on the departure on his Blogger account, entirely different from the band's response, claiming that the band was "a manufactured product of a major-label." He further accused Hayley Williams of being manipulated by her management, treating the rest of the group as her solo project, and claimed she was the only member of the band who was signed to Atlantic Records, while her bandmates were simply "riding on the coattails of her dream".

On December 30, 2010, MTV News interviewed Williams, York and Davis in Franklin, Tennessee regarding their reactions to Farro's response. The interview aired on MTV.com on January 7, 2011 as *Paramore: The Last Word*. While the band confirmed many of Farro's statements, notably that Williams was indeed the only member of the band actually signed to Atlantic, they said they felt the statement was irrelevant, adding that they had addressed many of the claims made already throughout the course of their career.

2011–present: Paramore without the Farro brothers

On January 10, 2011, in an interview with MTV, Hayley Williams has said that despite the band losing two of its founding members, they will be releasing new music in 2011, though it is not known yet if they will manage to record a full album for release this year, or just release some songs. The singer also admitted that Paramore's style was likely to change with the new lineup, but clarified that the band would still retain their signature sound.

On February 2, 2011, Josh Farro confirmed the name of his new band, Novel American. Zac has also confirmed his new band, Half Noise.

On February 17, 2011, Hayley Williams has confirmed that the band will be hitting the studio upon returning from their South American tour, to record a batch of songs to be released over the summer, prior to a new full-length album that might follow late this year or in 2012. One of the new songs to be released include "In the Mourning", which Williams debuted on her Tumblr page.

On March 21, 2011, Paramore stated on their various social networking accounts that they were entering a studio in Los Angeles with producer Rob Cavallo to record their next album.

On June 3, 2011, Paramore released the single "Monster", featured on the *Transformers: Dark of the Moon* soundtrack, on Youtube. This is the first song that the band released without the Farro brothers.

On June 9, 2011, Hayley Williams announced that the band are starting to write their fourth album, which they hope to start recording at the end of the year, so it'll be ready for release in early 2012.

Musical style and influences

Paramore's music has generally been regarded as "emo" and "pop punk". Joshua Martin had written after an interview with Hayley Williams, "The band isn't just a short pop-punk girl with red hair and a spunky attitude. Their music is like them, it's aged differently. It's sped up, and slowed down. It's emo without being whiny, or bratty. Almost a very literal anti-Avril Lavigne." *Alternative Press* magazine had commented that the band was "young sounding", while consistently being "honest."

Paramore's first album *All We Know is Falling* had an arguably more "formulaic pop-punk" sound that was "delivered particularly well" and the combination of the two had created a "refined rock infused pop/punk album." The band's second release, *Riot!* was said to explore a 'diverse range of styles," however, not straying far from "their signature sound."

Alternative Press and various other reviewers have noted that the band's stage performances have helped boost them to larger fame. *Alternative Press* states that Williams "has more charisma than singers twice her age, and her band aren't far behind in their chops, either." Singer-songwriter John Mayer had praised Williams' voice in a blog in October 2007, calling her "The great orange hope"; "orange" in reference to her hair color. Due to the female fronted aspect of the band, Paramore has gained comparisons to Kelly Clarkson and the aforementioned Avril Lavigne, to which one reviewer said was "sorely unfounded." Reviewer Jonathan Bradley noted that "Paramore attacks its music with infectious enthusiasm." However, he also explained that "there isn't a whole lot of difference between *Riot!* and the songs from Kelly Clarkson or Avril Lavigne." A reviewer at *NME* had likened Paramore's sound to that of "No Doubt (stripped of all the ska bollocks)" and "Kelly Clarkson's wildest dreams." Hayley Williams has gone on to comment about the female aspect of the band saying that Paramore is not "this girl-fronted band" and it makes "music for people to enjoy music, not so people can talk about my sexuality."

Paramore has expressed appreciation for Fall Out Boy, Panic! at the Disco, Blink-182, Death Cab for Cutie, Jimmy Eat World, MewithoutYou, and Sunny Day Real Estate, as well as Thrice and New Found Glory; Hayley Williams citing her personal influences as Robert Smith of The Cure and Etta James. Williams also explained that bands such as U2, "who are massive, and do whatever they want, write whatever they want and they stand for something," Jimmy Eat World, "who I don't think ever disappoint their fans," and No Doubt, who "have done amazing things," act as a pattern for the path in which Paramore would like to take their career.

In an interview with the BBC, Josh Farro stated "Our faith is very important to us. It's obviously going to come out in our music because if someone believes something, then their world view is going to come out in anything they do. But we're not out here to preach to kids, we're out here because we love music."

Current members
- Jeremy Davis – bass guitar (2004, since 2005)
- Hayley Williams – lead vocals, keyboards, piano (since 2004)
- Taylor York – lead and rhythm guitars, glockenspiel, percussion (since 2007)

Current touring members
- Josh Freese – drums (since 2010)
- Jon Howard – rhythm guitar, keyboards, piano backing vocals (since 2010)
- Justin York – guitars, backing vocals (since 2010)

Former members
- Josh Farro – lead guitar, backing vocals (2004–2010)
- Zac Farro – drums, percussion (2004–2010)
- Hunter Lamb – rhythm guitar (2005–2007)
- Jason Bynum – rhythm guitar, backing vocals (2004–2005)
- John Hembree – bass guitar (2005)

Discography
Studio albums
- *All We Know Is Falling* (2005)
- *Riot!* (2007)
- *Brand New Eyes* (2009)

Awards
Among other awards, Paramore has been nominated for three Grammy Awards.

Appearances in video games
In 2005, Paramore made its first video game appearance with the song "Pressure" being featured in the console versions of the video game *The Sims 2*.

In March 2008, Paramore made its first rhythm game appearance with "Crushcrushcrush" as a downloadable track in the *Rock Band* games and later being a playable song in *Guitar Hero On Tour: Decades*. Later that year, *Rock Band 2* was released with the song "That's What You Get" included as a playable track. The video game *Guitar Hero World Tour* featured the song "Misery Business" along with Hayley Williams participating in motion capture sessions for the game. She is featured as an unlockable character in the game as well.

"Misery Business" is also featured in *Saint's Row 2*, and the soundtrack for *EA Sports NHL 08*.

The music video for "Decode", along with the *Twilight* film trailer, was shown in the North American *Home Theater* of PlayStation Home from December 11, 2008 to December 18, 2008. Source (edited): "http://en.wikipedia.org/wiki/Paramore"

Paramore's Videos. All of Them. Ever

Paramore's Videos. All of Them. Ever was released on May 11, 2010, and features 10 of Paramore's most popular videos.

Music videos
- "The Only Exception" (Directed by Brandon Chesbro)
- "Brick by Boring Brick" (Directed by Meiert Avis)
- "Ignorance" (Directed by Honey)
- "Decode" (Directed by Shane Drake)
- "That's What You Get" (Original Version) (Directed by Marcos Siega)
- "Crushcrushcrush" (Directed by Shane Drake)
- "Misery Business" (Directed by Shane Drake)
- "Emergency" (Directed by Shane Drake)

- "Pressure" (Directed by Shane Drake)
- "All We Know" (Directed by Dan Dobi)

Source (edited): "http://en.wikipedia.org/wiki/Paramore%27s_Videos._All_of_Them._Ever"

2010 Summer Tour EP

Summer Tour EP is an EP by American rock band Paramore that was sold during the 2010 Honda Civic Tour and the tour supporting their previously released album *Brand New Eyes*.

Personnel
- Hayley Williams - lead vocals
- Josh Farro - lead guitar
- Jeremy Davis - bass guitar
- Zac Farro - drums
- Taylor York - rhythm guitar

Source (edited): "http://en.wikipedia.org/wiki/2010_Summer_Tour_EP"

All We Know Is Falling

All We Know Is Falling is the debut studio album by American rock band Paramore, released on July 26, 2005. The album reached #8 on the UK Rock Chart. In the USA, it reached #30 on the *Billboard*'s Heatseekers Chart but failed to chart on the Billboard 200.

According to Paramore's A&R at Atlantic Records, Steve Robertson, instead of giving the debut album a major radio promotional push, he believed the band should start small and slowly build through word of mouth. In his words, Robertson "wanted kids to discover the band without it being shoved down their throats."

As stated by singer Hayley Williams, the shadow on the sofa on the album art is meant to represent current bassist Jeremy Davis leaving the band. Davis temporarily left the band shortly after arriving in Orlando, Florida to record the album. Davis stated that he immediately regretted leaving and was overjoyed when the band asked him back shortly after the album's release. His departure had a large impact on the band, inspiring the song "All We Know", and thus the title of the album, "All We Know Is Falling". As of April 2009, the album has managed to sell 405,110 copies in the United States, though prior to *Riot!* being released the album had only sold 50,000 copies. On May 26, 2009, a deluxe edition of the album was released exclusively on iTunes with 2 live tracks and 3 music videos.

In September 2005, a special Japanese release containing the previously unreleased "Oh, Star" was made available.

Track listing
All lyrics written by Hayley Williams, except where noted, all music composed by Hayley Williams & Josh Farro, except when noted.

Paramore
- Hayley Williams – lead vocals
- Josh Farro - Lead Guitar
- Zac Farro - Drums and percussion
- Jason Bynum - Rythmn Guitar (2004 - 2005)
- John Hembree - Bass Guitar (2005)
- Hunter Lamb - Rythmn Guitar (2005)

Additional Musicians
- Lucio Rubino - bass guitar, except on "Here We Go Again"
- Jeremy Caldwell - bass guitar on "Here We Go Again"

Production
- James Paul Wisner - producer on "All We Know, "Never Let This Go" and "My Heart"
- Mike Green - producer on "Pressure", "Emergency", "Brighter", "Whoa", "Conspiracy" and "Franklin"; mixer, except on "Here We Go Again"
- Roger Alan Nichols & Nick Trevisick - producers & mixers on "Here We Go Again"
- Tom Baker - mastering engineer

Source (edited): "http://en.wikipedia.org/wiki/All_We_Know_Is_Falling"

Live in the UK 2008

Live in the UK 2008 is a live album by American rock band Paramore. The album is limited edition, with only a small number released featuring 3 live performances in Manchester, Brixton and Birmingham. It is believed that only 1000 copies of this release were made. Originally, there was going to be an option at each of the concerts to choose which live album could be bought. This was changed to only the Manchester live album being available at each of the dates. Brixton and Birmingham live albums had to be bought by February 5.

Fans could either pre-order the album online via Concert Live or buy the album at the concert itself. There was an option to buy the album by itself, or to buy it with the re-release of the "Misery Business" single in the UK. The first 200 who pre-ordered the album with the singles online received a signed version of the "Misery Business" single, while buying the singles at a concert meant each person had a 1 in 5 chance of receiving a signed copy.

Track listing
All songs written and composed by Paramore.

Trivia

- At the end of "Here We Go Again", a section of At the Drive-In's "One Armed Scissor" is covered on each of the live albums. This cover has been used at almost all of Paramore's live performances.
- Paramore performed a cover of "Sweetness" by Jimmy Eat World in the UK Riot! Tour, however, due to licensing rights, this song was not added to any of the live albums.
- The band thanks the three support bands who performed before them, which are New Found Glory, Kids in Glass Houses and Conditions.
- "Decoy" and "Misery Business" are both encore performances.

Source (edited): "http://en.wikipedia.org/wiki/Live_in_the_UK_2008"

Paramore discography

The discography of Paramore, an American alternative rock band, consists of three studio albums, three extended plays, two live albums, fourteen singles, one video album, and thirteen music videos. The band was formed in Franklin, Tennessee, in 2004 by lead vocalist Hayley Williams with bassist Jeremy Davis, guitarist Josh Farro, drummer Zac Farro and rhythm guitarist Taylor York. In 2005, Paramore signed with the New York City-based Fueled by Ramen and released their debut album entitled *All We Know Is Falling*. Three singles were released from the album but none of them charted. The album did not chart in the Billboard 200 either, although it peaked at number thirty in the *Billboard* Top Heatseekers. *All We Know Is Falling* also received a Gold certification in the United Kingdom.

The band's breakthrough album came in 2007 with *Riot!*. After its release in June, the album peaked at number fifteen on the *Billboard* 200 album chart and received multiple certifications all over the world, including a Platinum in the United States. The lead single, "Misery Business", became their first charting single in the Billboard Hot 100 and certified single. Paramore contributed to the *Twilight* film soundtrack in 2008 recording of two original songs, including the single "Decode".

In 2009, the band released their third studio album *Brand New Eyes*, which debuted and peaked at number two in the United States and became a number one album in several countries, including Australia and the United Kingdom. The album has produced five singles, including the lead "Ignorance" and the acoustic "The Only Exception", and received Gold certifications in numerous countries.

References

General

- "Paramore < Discography". *AllMusic*. Macrovision. Retrieved 2009-12-18.
- "Paramore: Discography". *Paramore.net*. Fueled by Ramen. Retrieved 2010-06-06.

Specific

External links

- Official website

Source (edited): "http://en.wikipedia.org/wiki/Paramore_discography"

Riot!

Riot! is the second studio album by American rock band Paramore, succeeding their debut album *All We Know Is Falling*, and was released in the United States on June 12, 2007 and in the United Kingdom on June 25, 2007. The album was certified Platinum in July 2008 by the Recording Industry Association of America (RIAA), and Gold in the UK. *Riot!* produced 4 singles: "Misery Business", "Hallelujah", "Crushcrushcrush" and "That's What You Get".

"Misery Business" is included in the video games *Saints Row 2*, *NHL 08*, *Rock Band 3* and *Guitar Hero World Tour* (the latter featuring a computer-generated replica of lead vocalist Hayley Williams), while "That's What You Get" is included as a playable song on *Rock Band 2*. "Crushcrushcrush" is featured on *Guitar Hero On Tour: Decades* and is available as a downloadable track for play on the three *Rock Band* games. A cover version of the song is also featured on the game *Ultimate Band*. The album cover also resembles the cover artwork of No Doubt's album Rock Steady. Riot went Platinum on July 11, 2008.

Music

Recording and production

The album was produced by David Bendeth. Lead vocalist, Hayley Williams, explained the album was called *Riot!* because, "For us, the title '*Riot!*' literally means an unbridled outburst of emotions. When we were writing, it seemed like our thoughts and emotions were coming out so fast that we couldn't control them. It felt like there was a riot within us. So the album takes our passion to a new level; it's just all raw energy."

The track "For a Pessimist, I'm Pretty Optimistic" comes from what lead guitarist Josh Farro reflects as "putting your faith in someone and they blow it." Farro composed the song and gave the demo to Williams. Farro is known as saying "I wrote the music specifically to be awesome live and to be extremely energetic. It all came out at once. I showed it to Hayley and she just nailed it lyrically. She completely got the feeling I wanted the song to have."

During production, Paramore held an online contest entitled "The Last Song You'll Ever Sing" where fans submitted videos on YouTube for the opportunity to sing back-up vocals on the track "Born for This". The winner was Mary Bonney of McLean, Virginia.

Songs

The album has yielded four singles, with "Misery Business" being the first. Its origins came from a message Williams posted on the band's LiveJournal, asking fans to post what they're ashamed of. "I found that people really were reaching out to someone to spill their guts to," she recalls, "so I did the same thing lyrically in the song and let everything out. It's more honest than anything I've ever written, and the guys matched that emotion musically." The song became an instant hit, eventually receiving heavy rotation on MTV and other music television networks.

The album's second single was "Hallelujah". As Williams recounts, "It's one of the oldest songs we've got, but we wanted to save it for this record, and it's the perfect home for it. It's a claim of victory for both ourselves and our fans."

The album's third single was "Crushcrushcrush" and was released January 15, 2008, in the US and the January 23 in the UK.

The album's fourth single, "That's What You Get", was released just over a week after Paramore canceled their European tour to work on "personal issues", amidst media speculation of the band breaking up. Williams explained that, given the fragile state of the band, they all thought it best if they kept the shoot low-key, surrounding themselves with their friends and family, keeping it simple. Williams added, "We had tons of friends there, and it really just felt like a hangout session. And Marcos [Siega, the director] was so cool about it. He said, 'Bring your friends.' We shot it in some of our friends' houses, and it just felt so real... and I think it's the first time in a video you're gonna get to see who we really are."

The track "Born for This" contains the line "we want the airwaves back", from the song "Liberation Frequency" taken from the album *The Shape of Punk to Come* by the influential Swedish hardcore band Refused. Williams has explained that this song was written "about the fans" and "that the whole pre-chorus is actually inspired by that one line of the song."

Release

Riot! was released in the United States on June 12, 2007, following the debut of "Misery Business" on the radio. It entered the U.S. *Billboard* 200 albums chart at 20 in late 2007. *Riot!* sold 42,000 albums in the U.S. in its first week and three months later the album hit its peak at 15 on the Billboard 200. The album achieved some success in the UK reaching #24 on the albums chart sales to date 250,094. The album was certified Platinum on July 11, 2008. The hit single "Misery Business" has also been certified Platinum by the RIAA. The album was re-released in late 2007 as a U-MYX MVI CD/DVD. In New Zealand, the album peaked at number 15, and was certified Gold on February 1, 2009, shipping over 15,000 copies. Critical opinion for *Riot!* was mixed. Some critics gave the album positive reviews; Jason Lymangrover of Allmusic gave the album 4 out of 5 stars and commented that, "Ultimately, this disc has enormous crossover potential, and will probably appeal to those who are fans of the genre, and for those who aren't, there's a good chance of it becoming a guilty pleasure." Stylus Magazine gave the album a B+ and said, "*Riot!* is immediately appealing because it focuses on sounds that have been neglected by the genre's front-runners. This is an uncomplicated album of strikingly uncomplicated music, entirely lacking in 15 word song titles." Gareth Dobson of Drowned in Sound gave the album 4 out of 10 stars and said, "At 38 minutes long, it's mercifully brief, but still manages to feel like a double album for those who endure it. That is, those who don't manage to forget that it's on the stereo at all. People, get your pop-punk thrills somewhere else. At least somewhere where there are actual thrills to be had." Despite mixed and lukewarm reviews, *Riot!* found itself in several "must have" lists that were compiled by various music publications, networks and other media.

Riot! Tour

Williams said, "We're hoping to do one more tour across the States before we really get started with all the (European summer) festivals. Of course, I want to do more Warped Tour dates, 'cause it's, like, my favorite tour ever. We'll see what works out and hopefully just have another great year."

After the album release the band went on an American tour, following it up with a world tour. After their fourth single from *Riot!* was released the band canceled their European tour to work on "personal issues."

Track listing

All songs written and composed by Hayley Williams and Josh Farro, except where noted.

Personnel

- Hayley Williams – lead vocals
- Josh Farro – lead guitar, rhythm guitar, backing vocals
- Jeremy Davis – bass guitar
- Zac Farro – drums, percussion

Source (edited): "http://en.wikipedia.org/wiki/Riot!"

The Final Riot!

The Final Riot! is the second official live album by American rock band Paramore and was released on November 25, 2008 with a bonus DVD containing the full live concert plus behind-the-scenes footage.

The DVD was filmed on August 12, 2008, at the Congress Theater in Chicago on the The Final Riot! Summer Tour.

It contains a documentary entitled "40 Days of Riot!", showing the band on tour. It is available in a standard and limited deluxe edition, which includes a 36-color-page booklet of the tour, along with another documentary, *40 MORE Days of Riot!*

The Final Riot! was certified Gold by the RIAA on March 17, 2009, selling over 50,000 copies.

Track listing

All songs written and composed by Hayley Williams, Josh Farro and Taylor York.

Personnel

- Hayley Williams – lead vocals, keyboard
- Josh Farro – lead guitar, backing vocals
- Jeremy Davis – bass guitar
- Zac Farro – drums, percussion
- Taylor York – rhythm guitar, glockenspiel on "We Are Broken"

Source (edited): "http://en.wikipedia.org/wiki/The_Final_Riot!"

The Summer Tic EP

The Summer Tic EP is an EP by American rock band Paramore that was sold during the 2006 Warped Tour and the tour supporting their previously released album *All We Know Is Falling*. The name of the EP comes from a line in the song "Stuck on You", which is a cover of a song by Failure.

Track listing

All songs written and composed by Paramore except the song "Stuck on You" which is a cover of Failure. The "Crab mix" refers to the producer, who Zac Farro thought "moved like a crab" while playing ping pong. The song features the original screaming done by lead guitarist Josh Farro, which was removed for their album *All We Know Is Falling*.

Source (edited): "http://en.wikipedia.org/wiki/The_Summer_Tic_EP"

Brand New Eyes World Tour

Brand New Eyes World Tour is a series of American alternative rock concert tours by Paramore, touring North America, Europe, Asia, Japan, Australia, United Kingdom, South America, New Zealand and others.

Tour

Paramore announced their U.S. tour for *Brand New Eyes* on their official site, with The Swellers and Paper Route joining them as opening acts. The first show of the tour was played at a packed Fox Theater in Pomona, California, on September 29, 2009 (the day of the album's release). During "Decode", Williams lost her voice and the two remaining songs in the setlist were played instrumentally. The tour, which previously went from September 29, 2009, to November 1, 2009, was later officially postponed on October 2, 2009, due to a case of laryngitis for singer Hayley Williams. The full tour resumed on October 10, 2009, in Chicago.

The band also announced that they would be doing a European tour starting off in Helsinki, Finland, on November 29, 2009, with You Me at Six, Paper Route, and Now, Now Every Children supporting all UK tour dates.

They performed in February 2010 in the Australian Soundwave Festival, along with bands such as You Me at Six, Taking Back Sunday, All Time Low and Alexisonfire. They performed at the Soundwave Festival before they did the Brand New Eyes Tour in Australia. Then in the first week of march they performed two concerts in New Zealand. One to a sell out crowd of 5000 in Auckland and the other in Christchurch.

Paramore will support Green Day on their tour. They will open the concerts of Green Day in Dublin, Ireland (June 23, 2010) and in Paris, France (June 26, 2010).

In July, August and September 2010, the band announced a tour in the Honda Civic Tour 2010.

In May 2010, the band announced a short UK tour for November 2010.

In June 2010, the band announced a short Australia Tour for October

In November 2010, the band announced a short in South American Tour for February and March, and the band announced a short American tour for December

They have stated that after their South American tour, the band will take a break to write for their next album.

Honda Civic Tour Show

The Honda Civic tour was the biggest production the band had had so far. The stage was constructed of 3 ramps up to a platform behind the drum set, and 6 large video screens behind that. The show began with a large black curtain concealing the stage while the band played an instrumental intro, with spotlights revealing the silhouettes of the band. As the intro ended, they begin playing "Ignorance" as the curtain simultaneously dropped, the video screens flashing the band's logo during the intro, as the intro progressed the video screen changed to images of light bulbs (similar to the song's music video) during the intro, light bulbs also swung down from the top of the stage, continuing to swing throughout the song. The band then played "Feeling Sorry" as the video screens each showed a live feed of each member of the band performing during the choruses, at the end of the bridge the band would stop playing and Hayley would greet the crowd and welcome them to the tour. After playing "That's What You Get" and "Emergency" the band played "Playing God" as the video screens showed images of picture frames, the same picture frames on the back of Brand New Eyes and the song's single cover. After that they played Careful , as images of the Brand New Eyes butterfly flashed during the chorus, they then continued with their hit-single "Decode" as the video screen showed the band running through the forest with fireworks and flares, the video has been described as a part-two to the songs music video. After that Hayley Williams and Josh Farro moved to stage left and performed an acoustic cover of Loretta Lynn's "You Ain't Women Enough." After that, a red couch (similar to the one on the cover of All We Know is Falling) and a small lamp were brought out and the band performed a three song acoustic set, during this the light bulbs from Ignorance were brought down again to illuminate the stage. After that the band returned with "Let the Flames Begin" while the video screens showed images of open hands during the 'Oh Father' outro. They then performed "Crushcrushcrush" and "Pressure " stopping in the bridge during "Pressure" for Hayley to introduce all the band members, and for Josh to introduce Hayley. They then performed "Looking Up" while each of the video screens showed lyrics to the song and each of the band members daily lives, at the end of the song all the members came together to ride bikes as the split-screens faded away. They then ended their main set with their biggest hit "The Only Exception" as pyrotechnics were used during the last chorus of the song. The band then exited and come back for an encore, starting with "Brick By Boring Brick" while the video screens showed various images, including deserts, snakes, the Brand New Eyes butterfly, and hot air balloons. After "Brick" the band concluded their set with their breakthrough song "Misery Business" as flashing images of the "Riot!" logo filled the video screens, during the bridge Williams would let one, or sometimes various fans on stage to sing the rest of the song or sometimes play guitar, and as the last chorus came in confetti cannons were shot towards the crowd. The set concluded with the video screen showing Paramore's logo and the band bowing then leaving the stage. They used the same production for their Oceania and UK tours.

2009 Paramore Tours

Fall Tour

Paramore, Fall Tour 09.

Opening Acts

- Paper Route
- The Swellers (North America)
- You Me at Six (Europe)
- Now Now Every Children (Europe)
- AFI (Ulalume Festival at Merriweather Post Pavilion)
- Dead By Sunrise (Ulalume Festival at Merriweather Post Pavilion)
- Kid Cudi (Ulalume Festival at Merriweather Post Pavilion)

Setlist

Tour Dates

Williams with Paramore performing at the Brighton Centre, Brighton, UK on December 17, 2009.

2010 Paramore Tours

Pacific Run

Opening Acts

- You Me At Six (Australia)

Setlist

a This concert is a part of the Soundwave Festival

The Spring Tour

Opening Acts

- Relient K
- fun.

Setlist

Tour Dates

Paramore, The Spring tour.

European Festival & Concert Tour

Opening Acts
- The Blackout (Belfast)

Setlist
b Supporting Green Day.

Honda Civic Tour

Opening Acts
- Tegan and Sara
- New Found Glory
- Kadawatha
- Relient K (select dates only)

Setlist

Tour Dates

Paramore, The Honda Civic Tour.

c This concert is not a part of The Honda Civic Tour. It is part of the Reading and Leeds Festival weekend.

Oceania and Asia Tour

Opening Acts
- Relient K
- Jury and the Saints
- Yes2Kapitalism (Asia)

United Kingdom & Ireland Fall Tour

Opening Acts
- B.o.B (UK - England)
- All Forgotten (UK - Scotland)
- fun.
- Scuba Dice (Dublin)

Holiday Shows
d Hayley Williams only.
e The last show with Josh and Zac Farro.

2011 Paramore Tours

South American Tour

Opening Acts
- Locomotor (Peru)
- El sin sentido (Colombia)
- Cambio de Habito (Venezuela)
- Outono'09 (Brasilia)
- Alecto or Hey Ladies (Belo Horizonte)
- Fake Number (Rio de Janeiro) and (São Paulo)
- Doyoulike (Porto Alegre)
- Libra (Chile)
- The Avalanches (Puerto Rico)

MusiCares

Setlist
Source (edited): "http://en.wikipedia.org/wiki/Brand_New_Eyes_World_Tour"

Honda Civic Tour

The **Honda Civic Tour** is an annual concert tour, sponsored by Honda Motor Company which began in 2001. Each year, the headlining band or bands customize a Honda Civic for concert patrons to win in a raffle.

2001 Tour

First Half
- **Headliner:** blink-182
- **Supporting:** Alkaline Trio, No Motiv, Sum 41, and The Ataris

Second Half
- **Headliner:** Everclear
- **Supporting:** American Hi-Fi and The Mayfield Four

2002 Tour
- **Headliner:** Incubus
- **Supporting:** Hoobastank and Phantom Planet

2003 Tour
- **Headliner:** New Found Glory and Good Charlotte
- **Supporting:** Hot Rod Circuit, Less Than Jake, MXPX, Stretch Arm Strong, The Movielife, and The Disasters

2004 Tour
- **Headliner:** Dashboard Confessional
- **Supporting:** The Get Up Kids, Thrice, Val Emmich, The Format, Say Anything, Hot Water Music, Motion City Soundtrack and Head

Automatica

2005 Tour
- **Headliner:** Maroon 5
- **Supporting:** Phantom Planet, The Donnas and The Thrills

2006 Tour
- **Headliner:** The Black Eyed Peas
- **Supporting:** Flipsyde and The Pussycat Dolls

2007 Tour
- **Headliner:** Fall Out Boy
- **Supporting:** +44, The Academy Is.., Cobra Starship, and Paul Wall

2008 Tour
- **Headliner:** Panic! at the Disco
- **Supporting:** The Hush Sound, Motion City Soundtrack, and Phantom Planet

2009 Tour (Cancelled)
Originally planned for All-American Rejects and Jack's Mannequin to co-headline the tour, but it was cancelled.

2010 Tour
- **Headliner:** Paramore
- **Supporting:** Tegan and Sara (except on the July 28th show at the Comcast Center and the July 30th show in Norfolk Virginia, where Relient K performed), New Found Glory, Kadawatha

2011 Tour
- **Headliner:** blink-182 and My Chemical Romance
- **Supporting:** Rancid, Manchester Orchestra, Against Me!, Matt and Kim

Source (edited): "http://en.wikipedia.org/wiki/Honda_Civic_Tour"

Summer Tour 2009 (No Doubt)

The **Summer Tour 2009** is the fifth concert tour by American rock group, No Doubt.

Background

On December 3, 2008, the band announced on their official website plans of a tour and a new album . They stated, "As most of you saw from our little iChat (yes, it was really us), we have decided to go on tour next year while continuing to work on our album. We are working on tour dates now and can't wait to get out there and play for all of you - it's been too long! We'll announce tour dates soon so be sure to check back for updates. Have a safe and happy holiday and we'll see you on the road in 2009!"

The tour was officially announced in January 2009 by MTV News. Stefani cited the reason for tour was to perform their favorite songs and explore new musical directions. A survey on the band's website complied fan's favorite songs that have a possibility of being performed on the tour. During an interview with guitarist Tom Dumont, he explained the tour will have A Clockwork Orange theme, saying,

"Gwen came up with the Clockwork Orange thing—she started getting into the visuals of those modernist movies from the 60's. We've been looking at tons of art and it's like this space-age modernism from that decade—it's retro and modern at the same time, so we're building this crazy stage set that has that vibe. We have a bunch of really great artists doing t-shirts and posters that echo that. There's a whole look for the tour even though there's not an album yet."

It was also revealed that the group will give away their entire music catalog (in digital format) to spectators who purchased high level tickets. The group appeared on The Today Show, American Idol, The Ellen Degeneres Show, Jimmy Kimmel Live and Gossip Girl to promote the tour. This tour should not be considered a reunion tour, because No Doubt stated it is not a reunion since the band had never broken up.

Opening acts

No Doubt and Paramore performing in General Motors Place.

- Paramore (select dates)
- The Sounds (select dates)
- Bedouin Soundclash (select dates)
- Janelle Monae (select dates)
- Tinted Windows (band) (select dates)
- Katy Perry (select date)
- Panic! At The Disco (select dates)
- Matt Costa (select dates)

Setlist
- Spiderwebs
- Hella Good
- Underneath It All
- Excuse Me Mr.
- Ex-Girlfriend
- End It On This
- Simple Kind of Life
- Bathwater
- Guns of Navarone
- New
- Hey Baby
- Running
- Different People
- Don't Speak
- It's My Life
- Just A Girl

Encore
- Rock Steady
- Stand and Deliver
- Sunday Morning

a This concert is a part of the Bamboozle Festival
b This concert is a part of Tiger Jam XII

c This concert is a part of Summerfest
Source (edited): "http://en.wikipedia.org/wiki/Summer_Tour_2009_(No_Doubt)"

Hayley Williams

Hayley Nichole Williams (born December 27, 1988) is an American rock singer, songwriter and the lead vocalist of the band Paramore.

Life and career

In 2002, at the age of 13, Williams moved from her hometown, Meridian, Mississippi, to Franklin, Tennessee, where she met former band members Josh Farro and Zac Farro in school. Shortly after arriving, she began taking vocal lessons with Brett Manning. While still in school, she tried out for a local funk cover band called The Factory where she met Jeremy Davis.

Williams was discovered in 2003 by managers Dave Steunebrink and Richard Williams who signed the 14-year-old to a production deal. According to former manager Jeff Hanson in an interview with HitQuarters, at the time she was writing pop songs with top songwriters in Nashville. Williams was introduced to Atlantic Records A&R Tom Storms through Richard's attorneys Jim Zumwalt and Kent Marcus, and then signed to the label by Jason Flom. The label's original plan for their new artist was to make her a solo pop artist but Williams objected to this, saying that she wanted to be part of a band and play 'non-alternative rock' music. Atlantic decided to go along with her wishes and she then formed Paramore with Josh Farro, Zac Farro, and Jeremy Davis.

The music of Paramore was originally supposed to come out on Atlantic Records but the label's marketing department decided it would be better for the image of the band to not have them attached to a huge label. They instead released their music through a "cooler" niche label in Fueled by Ramen.

In 2007, Williams appeared in the music video for "Kiss Me" by New Found Glory.

In the 2007 *Kerrang!* Readers' Poll she finished second to Evanescence's Amy Lee in the "Sexiest Female" category, going on to win the first place spot for "Sexiest Female" a year later in the 2008 poll, and again in the 2009 poll. She also appears as a playable character in the video game *Guitar Hero World Tour*.

Williams wrote and recorded the song "Teenagers", which was featured in the soundtrack for the film *Jennifer's Body*. After the release of "Teenagers", Williams stated that she had no plans to establish herself as a solo artist. In 2010, she appeared on the tracks "Airplanes" and "Airplanes (Part II)" from alternative rapper B.o.B's debut album, *B.o.B Presents: The Adventures of Bobby Ray*. "Airplanes", later released as a single, peaked within the top ten in nineteen countries, including number one peak positions in the United Kingdom and New Zealand.

Paramore

Paramore was created in Franklin, Tennessee in 2004, with Williams (lead vocals/keyboards) alongside Josh Farro (lead guitar/backing vocals), Jeremy Davis (bass guitar) and Zac Farro (drums). Prior to forming Paramore, the other members of what was soon to be Paramore had been "edgy about the whole female thing" of having Williams as singer, but as they were good friends she began writing with them and eventually became a member. The band has released three studio albums, *All We Know Is Falling*, *Riot!*, and *Brand New Eyes* as well as two live albums and three EPs. In June 2009, the band welcomed Taylor York (rhythm guitar) as an official member, although he had already been playing as a touring member with the band since 2007.

In 2006, Paramore started touring outside of the US for the first time, which included a headline tour of the UK and supporting British post-hardcore rockband The Blackout on the Give It A Name Festival in Europe.

Source (edited): "http://en.wikipedia.org/wiki/Hayley_Williams"

Jeremy Davis

Jeremy Clayton Davis (born February 8, 1985) is an American bassist for the band Paramore.

Biography

Jeremy Davis was born on February 8, 1985 in North Little Rock, Arkansas. Davis is the bass player in the band Paramore . He has been playing bass for almost 14 years.

In 2002, at the age of 16, he was living in Franklin, Tennessee, where he played in a funk cover band called The Factory where he met Hayley Williams. Through Williams, Davis met the other members, brothers Josh Farro and Zac Farro. In 2005, John Janick, founder of record label Fueled by Ramen, signed a contract with them.

Davis also stated that his favorite bands are Deftones, Death Cab for Cutie, Thrice, Sigur Rós, Paper Route and Mew.

Paramore

Paramore was created in Franklin, Tennessee in 2004 by the two brothers Josh Farro (lead guitar/backing vocals) and Zac Farro (drums). Taylor York was also a part of the band from the very beginning, but his parents wanted him to finish school first. Later, they asked Hayley Williams (lead vocals/keyboards) to join the band, and, through Hayley, Jeremy Davis (bass guitar) joined as well. Prior to forming Paramore, the other members of what was soon to be Paramore had been "edgy about the whole female thing" of having Williams as singer, but as they were good friends she began writing with them and eventually became a member. The band was eventually signed to a deal on Fueled by Ramen. However, before they began recording, Davis left the band for unknown reasons. The song All We Know is about this. For this time, Davis was replaced by John Hembree. The band released their first album, All We Know Is Falling, and one EP, The Summer Tic, without him. However, he rejoined soon afterwards and was present on the band's second album, Riot!. Davis also plays bass on the live albums The Final Riot! and Live in the UK. The band's third album, *Brand New Eyes*, was released on September 29, 2009.

Equipment
Bass guitars
- Custom Fender Jazz Bass
- Fender Jazz Bass's
- 52' Vintage Fender Precision Bass
- 62' Vintage Fender Precision Bass

Effects
- Boss TU-2 Tuner (*Rumour*)
- V2 Angry Fuzz (*Rumour*)
- Russian Big Muff (*Rumour*)
- BOSS GEB-7 Bass Equalizer (*Rumour*)
- Big Muff Pi (*Rumour*)

Amps On the 2007 tour with Paramore, he was using a Sansamp DI, into an Ampeg SVT Classic head, through a Ampeg SVT810.
- Ampeg SVT810AV (*Rumour*)

Source (edited): "http://en.wikipedia.org/wiki/Jeremy_Davis"

Josh Farro

Joshua Neil Farro (born September 29, 1987) is an American rock guitarist and songwriter, and the lead guitarist of the band Novel American. He is best known as the former lead guitarist and backing vocalist of the alternative rock band Paramore. He is also the older brother of Paramore's former drummer, Zac Farro.

Paramore
Farro was a founding member and lead guitarist of Paramore from the band's creation in 2004 until 2010. Additionally, he provided backing vocals and was chiefly involved in writing almost all of the band's songs alongside Hayley Williams and Taylor York. On December 18, 2010, Paramore's official website announced that Farro and his brother Zac had decided to leave the band.

Departure and blog controversy
On December 21, a blog appeared online claiming to be an official exit statement from the Farro brothers. The blog was heavily critical of Williams' family, Atlantic Records and Fueled by Ramen. Additionally, it includes an alternate explanation of the band's formation, refuted statements made by the band's website announcement and regarding the brothers' departure, and negated previous claims that dissension amongst the band was healed during the writing of *Brand New Eyes*.

Despite the band's previous mention of fraudulent blogs regarding the event, Farro recently appeared in a video on YouTube claiming that the blog was genuine. The video has since been removed for reported violations of the website's sexual content policy. Farro re-uploaded the video a few days later.

In an interview with MTV, Farro said that after watching Paramore: The Last Word interviews, he simply disagreed with the band on a lot of things but wishes them the best for the future and only wants to move on for the sake of their fans.

Novel American
On February 2, 2011, Farro announced and established a Twitter account for his new band, Novel American. The band includes his high school friends Van Beasley, Tyler Ward and Ryan Clark, each formerly of the band Cecil Adora. Unlike in Paramore, Farro is relegating himself to guitar in the new project, saying "I never wanted to sing. My voice — and this is not false humility — is just not that good"

On Feb 22, 2011, the band announced Farro's brother Zac would replace Tyler Ward on drums.

Personal life
Farro was born in Voorhees Township, New Jersey on September 29, 1987. He is the second-oldest of his other four siblings, including former Paramore drummer Zac Farro. Farro is three quarters Italian. He is a self-taught guitarist, and began playing when he was 13 years old. On April 3, 2010 Farro married fiancee Jenna Rice in Tennessee, missing the band's Pacific Rim tour to plan the nuptials.

He plays guitar exceptionally well with brother Zac on the drum.

Musical influences
Farro's musical influences include Jimmy Eat World, Incubus, Underoath, Sunny Day Real Estate, Death Cab for Cutie, John Mayer, James Taylor, Sigur Ros and Mew.

Side projects
Josh has recorded unreleased solo tracks featuring Zac Farro and Hayley Williams. Tracks include:
- "Plane Crash Dreams" with Hayley Williams
- "I Had a Revelation"
- "So Much More"
- "Worry"

Equipment
Guitars
- Fender Telecaster Thinline
- Fender Telecaster Deluxe
- Fender Jazzmaster
- Fender Stratocaster
- Gibson Les Paul
- Burns London Double Six 12-string

guitar (Studio - bridge of "Brick by Boring Brick")
- Taylor Acoustic

Amps
- Marshall JCM2000 Dual Super Lead head (Along with a Marshall 1960A Angled 4x12 Cab)
- Mesa Boogie Dual Rectifier
- Marshall JTM 45 (Studio - bridge of "Brick by Boring Brick")

Effects
- BOSS Chromatic Tuner
- BOSS DD-20 Giga Delay (x2)
- Digitech Whammy
- Ernie Ball Volume Pedal Jr.
- Keeley Katana Boost pedal (used on "Turn It Off")
- Voo Doo Labs power supply

Misc
- Mogami and George L Cables

- D'Addario EXL110 Regular Light 10-46 Gauge guitar strings (listed on D'Addario as being a user, beginning in 2009), previously a user of Ernie Ball strings.
- Sennheiser ew372 G2 wireless

Source (edited): "http://en.wikipedia.org/wiki/Josh_Farro"

Taylor York

Taylor Benjamin York (born December 17, 1989) is an American rock guitarist and is currently a member of the alternative rock band Paramore. He also plays the keyboard and glockenspiel occasionally during their live set. His brother is Justin York, a touring member of Relient K.

Biography

Taylor York was born on December 17, 1989 in Nashville, Tennessee. He was the rhythm guitarist in the band Paramore, however, after the departure of Zac and Josh Farro he is now the lead guitarist. His brother is Justin York who is a member of Cecil Adora. Taylor's father is Peter York (a music executive at Sparrow Records) who also is a skilled guitarist, taught both Justin and Taylor the instrument. York had been in a band with the Farro brothers (Josh Farro and Zac Farro) before the two met Hayley Williams, and originally took part in writing songs such as Conspiracy from their debut album, All We Know Is Falling. York had played with Paramore as a touring member for two years (2007–2009) but was never an actual member, until it was announced on June 15, 2009 through the band's Livejournal that he was now an official member of the band.

Influences

York also stated that his favorite bands include mewithoutYou, Radiohead, Jimmy Eat World, Yann Tiersen, At the Drive-In, Bjork, Kadawatha and Paper Route.

Paramore

Taylor began playing rhythm guitar live for Paramore after the departure of Hunter Lamb. In the liner notes for the group's second album, *Riot!*, Hayley Williams, Josh Farro, Zac Farro and Jeremy Davis all included him on their list of 'thank-you's.

After the release of *Riot!*, Paramore released a live album, *The Final Riot*. While Taylor plays on this record, he is credited as a member of the band.

In June 2009, Taylor was officially acknowledged by Paramore as a rhythm/lead guitarist and took part in writing on their album *Brand New Eyes*.

His brother, Justin York, temporarily filled in for Josh Farro as lead guitar during Paramore's Pacific Tour and will be for Paramore's South American Tour.

Source (edited): "http://en.wikipedia.org/wiki/Taylor_York"

Zac Farro

Zachary Wayne Farro (born June 4, 1990) is an American musician and drummer of the bands Novel American and Half Noise. He is best known as the former drummer of the alternative rock band Paramore from its inception until 2010. He is the younger brother of Josh Farro, the band's former lead guitarist.

Personal life

Born in Voorhees Township, New Jersey, Zac is the middle child of five siblings (Nate, Joshua, himself, Jonathan, and Isabelle) and is of Italian descent. Zac began playing drums at around the age of nine, and he was eleven years old when he played his first drum kit.

Influences

Some of his favorite bands include: Jimmy Eat World, Radiohead, Death Cab for Cutie, Mew, Paper Route, Sigur Ros, Thrice, Sunny Day Real Estate and múm. Farro has been influenced by Dave Grohl (former drummer of Nirvana and current singer/songwriter of Foo Fighters and drummer for Them Crooked Vultures), William Goldsmith (former drummer of Sunny Day Real Estate and Foo Fighters, replaced by Taylor Hawkins) and Riley Breckenridge (drummer for the band, Thrice). His favorite songs to perform live are "Misery Business", "My Heart" and "For a Pessimist, I'm Pretty Optimistic". In a video for Gretsch Drums Zac Farro stated that he likes to play "Decode" and "Let The Flames Begin".

Paramore

Farro was a founding member of Paramore, created in Franklin, Tennessee in 2004, with Hayley Williams (lead vocals/keyboards), his brother Josh Farro (lead guitar/backing vocals) and Jeremy Davis (bass guitar). Jeremy Davis admitted he was initially unsure if the band could be taken seriously because of Zac's young age until he saw him play. The band released three studio albums, *All We Know Is Falling*, *Riot!* and *Brand New Eyes*, as well as two live albums and one EP. *Brand New Eyes*, their third album, was released on September 29, 2009. In June 2009, the band welcomed Taylor York (rhythm guitar), a long time friend of the Farros' and who previously played with them as a touring member. On December 18, 2010 the band's website announced the Farros' amicable departure. On December 21, 2010, Josh Farro released an official exit statement for himself and his brother, refuting the band's previous story.

Half Noise

Two days after his departure from Paramore, Zac took part in a new project band called "Tunnel", releasing a new song called "Hide Your Eyes". The duo then renamed themselves "Half Noise" due to other bands being named "Tunnel". The band features Farro (drums, vocals) and Jason Clark (guitar, vocals).

Farro and Clark had earlier been together in a band with Taylor York and Josh Farro.

Novel American

Josh Farro founded the band Novel American with former Cecil Adora members Van Beasley, Ryan Clark and Tyler Ward briefly after his departure from Paramore and the group announced plans to record an EP as well as play local venues in the near future.

On Feb 22, 2011, the band announced Zac Farro will replace Tyler Ward on drums.

Gear

Zac is currently endorsing Gretsch Drums, Pro-Mark sticks, Zildjian cymbals and Remo drum heads. He was previously sponsored by Truth Custom Drums and Meinl Percussion. He has two drum kits,(one is in Europe and one is in America) both are Gretsch. One is a black marine nitron wrap (American). The other is a Champagne sparkle wrap (European).

Cymbal Setup:
- 22" K Dark Medium Ride
- (2) 22" K Ride (as crashes)
- And a hihat combination of a 15" K Light Hi Hat Bottom (used as a top) and a 15" A New Beat Bottom

Occasionally his Hats have been the pairs of either 15" K Light Hats and 15" New Beat Hats. He has also used a Zildjian 21" Sweet Ride in Traditional finish as a crash from time to time.

Side Project

Zac has recorded tracks outside of Paramore by himself and with Josh Farro. These songs were never released. Tracks include:
- Far
- Kings
- Nothing New

Source (edited): "http://en.wikipedia.org/wiki/Zac_Farro"

All We Know

"**All We Know**" is a song by American rock band Paramore. It was released on December 26, 2006 in the United Kingdom, and February 26, 2007 in the United States from their debut album, *All We Know Is Falling*. It was written by Hayley Williams, and is about the departure of the band's bassist, Jeremy Davis.

Background

The song is about the departure of the band's bass player, Jeremy Davis, and the divorce of Hayley Williams' parents.

Reception

The only given review of the song is by *Digital Spy*, who awarded the album an adequate 3 out 5 stars, saying, ""The song slides from hard-rocking, crashing guitars and emotive, angry vocals to a much softer sound to start off the last third of the song, and Williams' vocals really do stand out on 'All We Know', her voice almost trilling as she hits the high notes and yelping out that "it takes some time to let you go" before Paramore take us to a much gentler interlude, swiftly followed by a return to this group's fast-paced sound."

Music video

A music video directed by Dan Dobi was filmed during their American tour and features clips of the band performing the song live at several locations.
Source (edited): "http://en.wikipedia.org/wiki/All_We_Know"

Brick by Boring Brick

"**Brick by Boring Brick**" is a song by American rock band Paramore, and the second single from their third album *Brand New Eyes*. "Brick by Boring Brick" was also featured in *The Vampire Diaries* episode "Under Control" that aired on April 15, 2010. In terms of airplay, it is one of the album's successful singles, including the song "The Only Exception."

Reception

The song received a positive review from Alex Fletcher of *Digital Spy*, who gave the song 4 stars out of 5. He said the song is "infectious, deliciously dark ('Well go get your shovel, and we'll dig a deep hole'), and packed with more energy than a Jedward dance routine – Williams sounds downright tremendous leading the 'ba-ba-ba' climax – this should provide a welcome edge at the top end of the charts". Rolling Stone stated that "Brick by Boring Brick" was able to "weave unexpected Smashing Pumpkins-style sonics into the mix." The song received a positive review from Vicki Lutas of the *BBC*, who awarded the song 5 out of 5 stars. She said that the song is "hair-raisingly BRILLIANT" and said "Listening to the lyrics is like entering a world where sandcastles aren't built, but buried, a world where the baddie is not the wolf, but reality... and in this world, things are dark, but they're very real. There's a sense of longing; longing for those fairy tales and longing for innocence, but it's coupled with a sense of realization that this will never happen." It talks about fuzzy bears and tooth picks, which are Hayley's favourite things in the world.

Music video

The music video for "Brick by Boring Brick" was filmed in Los Angeles on October 8, 2009. It was co-directed by Meiert Avis and Chris LeDoux (New Found Glory, U2). The video depicts a young girl (Harley Graham) with butterfly wings exploring a surreal landscape, while Hayley sings the song near a large ditch which guitarist Josh Farro is digging. Eventually the little girl's fantasy world becomes dark and frightening, with the character she was friends with before now turning into dark and sinister creatures, and she runs to escape, picking up her doll, emerging into the sunlight and falling into the ditch by where Hayley is singing. Hayley stands up and throws the girl's doll in after her, and Josh (out of the shot) throws the first shovelful of earth into the ditch.

In an interview with MTV, bassist Jeremy Davis explained that the band had created a treatment for the video before receiving further ideas from several directors. The video is Paramore's first to not be performance based and some of the members of the band are only seen for a short period of time. It is their first video to be filmed in front of green screen, and to have "a whole story behind it", with acting. Guitarist Josh Farro likened the video to the 2006 Spanish fantasy film *Pan's Labyrinth*. It was originally set to premiere on November 17 on *The Hills*, but was later postponed. The video was eventually released on Paramore.net on November 23.

Live performances

The track has been performed by Paramore on many occasions. The band's first performance of the song was in July 2009. Paramore performed a live version of "Brick By Boring Brick" for *MTV Unplugged*. For the performance, Williams wore a black dress with her hair down, while other members of the band dressed in causal clothing, such as jeans, t-shirts and knitted hats. It was also performed at the Ulalume Festival

The song was performed as the last song on the bands fall tour in October to December 2009. At the end of the song, the support groups would join the band on stage.

The band performed the song on *Late Night with Jimmy Fallon* on the 29th of April 2010.

Appearances

Brick By Boring Brick was used in *The Vampire Diaries*, in the 18th episode of season one titled 'Under Control'.

Irish pop punk band, TheElement have covered this song on live performances around Europe.

Source (edited): "http://en.wikipedia.org/wiki/Brick_by_Boring_Brick"

Careful (Paramore song)

"**Careful**" is a song by the American rock band Paramore, and is the fourth single from their third studio album, *Brand New Eyes*. The song charted on the *Billboard* Hot 100 the week *Brand New Eyes* was released before it was announced as a single. It charted due to digital downloads. Several radio websites announced this as an upcoming US single.

Music video

It was announced on the official Paramore fanclub that a video containing live footage of the song would be released on June 8, 2010. The video was shot and edited by Brandon Chesbro, who also directed the video for the band's previous single "The Only Exception". The video was released via Fueled by Ramen's YouTube account. It contains performances of the song in many concerts throughout 2009 and includes clips from their Brisbane Soundwave Tour and also at their one-off performance at Festival Hall in Melbourne, Australia. The clip also contains footage from their 2010 Spring Tour as well as their 2009 Fall Tour. It also shows clips of the band off stage. The music video is also the third of Paramore's videos to be a compilation of performances from various concerts, the first two being "All We Know" from *All We Know Is Falling* and "Hallelujah" from *Riot!*.

Source (edited): "http://en.wikipedia.org/wiki/Careful_(Paramore_song)"

Crushcrushcrush

"**Crushcrushcrush**" is a song by American rock band Paramore, and is the third single from their second studio album, *Riot!*. The official music video premiered on *TRL* on October 16, 2007. The single was released in late 2007 and early 2008. It was made available in the United Kingdom for download from November 5 and purchase on November 26, 2007. The single is also playable on various music video games such as *Rock Band*, *Rock Band Unplugged*, *Guitar Hero On Tour: Decades*, and *Ultimate Band*. The single won a Teen Choice Award for "Best Rock Track".

It was also used briefly in *NCIS*, in the episode "Stakeout".

The song was certified Gold in the United States on September 17, 2008.

Music video

The music video shows the band performing in a barren desert environment, and three people spying on them with binoculars from a distance. The three voyeurs watch from behind various old trinkets that have formed a faux house without walls or a roof. Intercut between Paramore's performance of the song are clips of the band walking through the voyeur's "house" and later on, short clips show that Paramore and the bandits watching them are the same (Hayley in the bathtub, Josh and Jeremy playing/slamming their guitars and Zac pushing his stands over and throwing drums). The video was directed by Shane Drake.

The music video is played throughout a television advertisement for the iPod Touch.

The video was also nominated for a Best Rock Video at the 2008 MTV Video Music Awards, but lost to Linkin Park's "Shadow of the Day".

Single release

The single is available in 3 formats. In addition to "Crushcrushcrush", certain vinyl releases feature live versions of "Misery Business" and "For a Pessimist, I'm Pretty Optimistic" from Paramore's album, *Riot!*

Source (edited): "http://en.wikipedia.org/wiki/Crushcrushcrush"

Decode (song)

"Decode" is a song by Paramore released as a single from the soundtrack to the film *Twilight*. It is also included as a bonus track on the international version of Paramore's third studio album, *Brand New Eyes*. An acoustic version of this song was released as a part of the special CD/DVD of the *Twilight* soundtrack. The song was certified Platinum in the U.S on February 16, 2010, selling over 1,000,000 copies. It was also nominated for a Grammy Award in 2010 for Best Song Written for a Movie.

Song information

Hayley Williams from Paramore is a *Twilight* fan and recently talked about her love of the books and the song's title:

> " *Twilight* is the first series of books I've ever read. I didn't get into the *Harry Potter* series, even though I love the movies. *Twilight* really caught my attention and held it. I'm really excited to see the book adapted to film and excited that our band gets to be a part of the phenomenon. I chose the title "Decode" because the song is about the building tension, awkwardness, anger and confusion between Bella and Edward. Bella's mind is the only one which Edward can't read and I feel like that's a big part of the first book and one of the obstacles for them to overcome. It's one added tension that makes the story even better."
>
> —Hayley Williams

Reception

Alexandra Cahill of Billboard.com gave the song a positive review by stating that "vocalist Hayley Williams captures the tension and urgency between undead protagonist Edward and mortal love interest Bella with an impassioned, yet restrained performance". Cahill also stated, "expertly crafted follow-up *Decode* promises to stake a claim at modern rock and top 40 radio".

Entertainment Weekly said that *Decode* took a step away from Paramore's "bouncier punk-pop sound for a more sprawling, Evanescence-like romanticism".

Music video

The official music video premiered on November 3, 2008 on MTVu, MTV, MTV2 and on MTV.com and was directed by Shane Drake. The video features the band members walking and performing in the woods, in Nashville, Tennessee (even though in the video, it is clearly supposed to be Forks, Washington). While they play, there are also scenes of the band acting as tracker vampires searching through the woods. Scenes from *Twilight* are also intercut.

The music video, along with the film trailer, were shown in the North American theater of Playstation Home from December 11, 2008 to December 18, 2008.

Chart performance

The song entered the U.S *Billboard* Hot Modern Rock Tracks at #35 and has peaked at #5, giving them their third top twenty hit on the chart. "Decode" became their second top forty hit, and their highest debut (#34) on the *Billboard* Hot 100. 7 weeks after its debut the song reached a new peak of #33. It also debuted at #52 on the Canadian Hot 100. It was only released digitally in the UK. The song was certified Platinum in the U.S on February 16, 2010, selling over 1,000,000 copies. In New Zealand, the song debuted at number #40 on November 24, 2009 and peaked at #15, becoming their highest peaking single there so far until the release of "The Only Exception". The song was certified Gold on July 5, 2009, selling over 7,500 copies, and spent a total of 15 weeks on the chart.

In Germany, the song debuted at number #50 on November 24, 2009 and peaked at #47 and spent a total of 9 weeks on the chart

Cover Versions

Joy Electric released a version of **Decode** on their 2009 cover album *Favorites at Play*.

Source (edited): "http://en.wikipedia.

org/wiki/Decode_(song)"

Emergency (song)

"**Emergency**" is a song by American rock band Paramore. It was released on October 21, 2006 as the first single from their debut album, *All We Know Is Falling*. It was released on 7" vinyl in the United Kingdom on August 26, 2006 and contained the B-side "Oh, Star," and a poster of the band. The song was written by Hayley Williams and Josh Farro. It failed to chart in the United States, however, it was released in *Kerrang!*s "Class of '06" compilation CD, calling it one of the best rock tracks of that year.

Background

The song is about the fact that love is taken for granted, and how most relationships are in emergency status. It is also about Williams' witnessing her parents' argument and failing marriage as a child. During an interview with the February 2008 edition of *Alternative Press*, Williams said,

> "I remember actually walking out the door with my mom that night and standing in between my parents and screaming "Shut up! Shut up! Shut up!"

Music Video

The music video features the band performing on a wooded stage.. all members of Paramore have either cuts, bruises and plasters on their faces. Halfway through the video you see the band in a small room talking. And at the end you see Hayley looking at a photo album with tears running down her cheeks

Source (edited): "http://en.wikipedia.org/wiki/Emergency_(song)"

Hallelujah (Paramore song)

"**Hallelujah**" is the second single from rock band Paramore's second album *Riot!*. The single peaked at #139 on the UK Singles Chart. The song is not to be confused with the Leonard Cohen song of the same name, although on the *Final Riot!* summer 2008 tour, lead singer Hayley Williams performs an extract, accompanied by lead guitarist, Josh Farro.

This song has two versions; the first one is the demo which got filtered and by that reason Hayley put all of her effort to make the new song better.

Music video

The video, directed by Big TV!, was officially released on July 30, 2007. The video appears as a photo montage of backstage and live performance photos, with the lyrics of the song written in the spaces between the photos. The video will zoom in and out on some of the photos. When the photo fills the entire screen, the photo will be revealed to actually be a short video clip, and the video clip will play. The video was shot at Rocketown in Nashville, USA when the band were playing their Riot! tour, even though the music is playing over the concert performance.

Single release

A CD single and two 7" vinyls were released in the UK on 10 September.

In other media

The song was featured in an episode of the British television soap opera *Hollyoaks* in October 2008 ("Misery Business" was also used in another episode in March 2008 and then later "Born for This" in September 2008). The song was also featured twice (once as a string quartet version) on the fourth season of *So You Think You Can Dance*.

Cover versions

The Rusty Pipes covered an a cappella version of the song (including Leonard Cohen's version) at their 13th Annual Pipe-A-Thon on December 12 2009, and posted it on their YouTube channel on January 24, 2010.

Source (edited): "http://en.wikipedia.org/wiki/Hallelujah_(Paramore_song)"

Ignorance (song)

"**Ignorance**" is a song by the American rock band Paramore. "Ignorance" was released by Fueled by Ramen in July 2009, as the lead single from the bands 2009 studio album entitled, *Brand New Eyes*. The single was written by Paramore band members Hayley Williams and Josh Farro; Paramore is also credited as being co-producers to the song. The track, recorded in Spring 2009, was the first song to be written for *Brand New Eyes*.

Musically, "Ignorance" is credited as being an alternative rock song. Williams' and Farros's inspiration for writing the song was from personal experiences. The track was generally well received by contemporary music critics. The song was commercially successful, charting within the top thirty in multiple territories, although the song performed better internationally. A music video for "Ignorance" was released in August 2009. In the video, the band is shown playing in a room with the only source of lighting being a hanging lightbulb.

Background

"Ignorance" was recorded by American Alternative band Paramore. The song was recorded in 2009. The track was written by Paramore's band members Hayley Williams and Josh Farro. It was released as the lead single from the band's 2009 studio album *Brand New Eyes* on July 7, 2009. James Montgomery of *MTV News* viewed the song as lyrically being about the "destructive nature of gossip, about the ugly, tear-'em-down world in which Paramore exist." "Ignorance" was the first song written for *Brand New Eyes*. In an interview with *Kerrang!*, Williams, who co-wrote the song, discussed the singles meaning, and her and Farro's inspiration for writing the song, saying,

"In my eyes, this song is a huge turning point for the band. The truth of it is, growing up is not easy. We're five different people who have to work towards the same goal on a daily basis. There were a lot of times when I felt really alone or angry or insecure. I don't always feel good at confronting people, especially people that I love, like these guys. Sometimes it takes songs to get the point across. The song is from one person's perspective. It's unfair that I'm the one who gets to talk about it but it helped me a lot. The line 'ignorance is your new best friend' is about how I felt I was losing people, and I think the band did too. But it's okay, we're growing up. I love that song."

Critical reception

"Ignorance" was generally well received by contemporary music critics. Leonie Cooper, a writer for *NME*, commented that "thankfully" Paramore's "new-found rage hasn't impinged on their talent for crafting a joyful pop song, as evidenced by the high octane" like "Ignorance", remarking that while the song "might be dark in tone" the song is still a "fairground-full of fun." A writer for *HitFix* gave the song a positive review, saying that while the single breaks no "new ground" for Paramore, it shows an "increased level of confidence" and "older Paramore fans will be happy to hear the Evanescence influence seems to be gone". Marc Hirsh, a writer from *The Boston Globe*, described the track as being a "thrilling little headlong rush."

Emily Steves, a writer for *Buffalo News*, noted that while "Ignorance" is a "harsh song fueled by Williams' passion to make her bandmates see and confront their problems" the song "proves to be one of their heaviest songs lyrically." Jon Canamanica, a writer for *The New York Times*, described the song as sounding more like a "muscular No Doubt song," with a "rhythmic shift" at the songs hook that "suggested a quick cough of ska." Ryan Wood, a writer for *The Nebraska City News Press*, strongly praised the track, commenting that the song "may go down" as the "best single ever." Scott Heisel, a writer for *Associated Press*, viewed the single as being a "sort of a 'roided out" version of Paramore's 2007 studio album *Riot!*'s song, "Misery Business" (2007). A writer for *Saffron Walden News* felt that the track displays Williams' "commendable and moody vocal range."

Chart performance

"Ignorance" had a good chart performance, generally charting within the top thirty. In the United States, the song performed worse than previous singles, peaking at number sixty seven on the *Billboard* Hot 100. It was more successful on other *Billboard* charts. The song's current peak position on the Hot Digital Songs Chart is number fifty eight; the song charted on the chart solely due to digital download sales. The track also charted on *Billboard*'s Rock Songs Chart, peaking at number twenty, as well as charting within the top ten on the Hot Modern Rock Tracks Chart, peaking at number seven. "Ignorance" had a better chart performance internationally. The single was successful in the United Kingdom, entering the chart within the top twenty at number fourteen, where it peaked. The track remained within the top 100 for seven weeks.

The song charted within the top twenty, peaking at number seventeen; the song remained on the chart for eight weeks. The single peaked at number thirty five in Australia; the song remained the on the countries chart for two weeks. The song had a similar chart performance in New Zealand, peaking at number thirty two and remained on the chart for five weeks. The track was less successful in Dutch, having entered the chart on October 18, 2009, at number eighty two, where it peaked, the following week the song fell out of the countries top 100. "Ignorance" was successful in Japan, charting within the top ten, peaking at number ten. The song also echoed similar chart success on Belgium's Singles Chart, peaking at number ten; it remained on the chart for four weeks. "Ignorance" is the first single by the band to chart on the Irish Top 50 Singles Chart, charting within the top fifty, peaking at number forty nine. It also charted at number forty two in Germany, as well as peaking at number ninety six on the Canadian Singles Top 100 chart.

Music video

The music video was released on August 13, 2009. The video begins with a door opening, showing Williams being singled out and ignored by other members of the band. She shines a light bulb that is hanging by a wire, directly in their faces, whilst describing how they ignore her and treat her like just another stranger in the lyrics. The cramped and bare setting emphasizes the inescapable, rising tensions between the band members. The video is intercut with clips of the band performing in a cramped small room, that appears to be a closet. Other clips show a larger performance area and a different personality of Williams being laid bare in white clothes, hair pulled back in the style like Björk's hair from her music video "Big Time Sensuality". It ends with the other members of the band being able to wrap the light bulb wire around Williams. James Montgomery of *MTV News* wrote that the video is "a claustrophobic, hard-charging thing that showcases Paramore: The Band. There is rumor that the band will be making a sequel music video, showcasing Hayley getting back at her band mates."

The sequel was probably Playing God (song).

Personnel

The following personnel contributed to "Ignorance":

References

Source (edited): "http://en.wikipedia.org/wiki/Ignorance_(song)"

List of Paramore songs

The following is a list of songs by the American alternative rock band Paramore.

Source (edited): "http://en.wikipedia.org/wiki/List_of_Paramore_songs"

Misery Business

"**Misery Business**" is a song by American rock band Paramore, and is the lead single from their second studio album, *Riot!*. "Misery Business" was the third Paramore video to be directed by Shane Drake, and was nominated for the "Best Video" award at the Kerrang! Awards 2007, but lost to Fall Out Boy's "This Ain't a Scene, It's an Arms Race".

This song is featured in the video games *Saints Row 2*, *NHL 08*, *Guitar Hero World Tour*, *Lips*, and *Rock Band 3*.

Chart performance

In the week ending June 25, 2007, "Misery Business" managed to debut at #99 on the *Billboard* Hot 100. "Misery Business" is the third charting single for the group in the United States, and the band's highest-charting airplay single to date. In the following week the song went up 13 positions to reach #86. Due to increased digital downloads during the month of August 2007, most notably during the latter half of the month, it re-entered the *Billboard* Hot 100 during the chart week of September 6, 2007 at #34, which was its peak until the chart week of January 5, 2008, when the song reached #31. Its current peak is #26. It also peaked at #3 on the Hot Modern Rock Tracks chart. The song was certified Platinum in the U.S on September 17, 2008, with over 1,000,000 digital downloads, and in December 2010 the song topped the 2 million mark in paid downloads. In Australia, in 2009, the song was certified Platinum. Selling over 15,000, in New Zealand, the Song was certified Gold on February 1, 2008, shipping over 7,500 copies.

The single was re-released in the UK Accorto Record Store on February 11, 2008 and included 3 vinyl records. It had been a success in many countries, like Latin America including Mexico, Argentina, Chile, Brazil and others.

The single, to date, has peaked at #17 on the UK Singles Chart. It is also the group's first charting single in the UK.

"Misery Business" has also debuted on the Dutch Top 40 peaking at #28 and in Finland at #23. It peaked on the German Top 40 at #12, which is the band's peak position in Germany.

Alternative Press named "Misery Business" Video of the Year in 2007.

Music video

The music video was filmed at Reseda High School in Reseda, California on December 21, 2006, and features a school and a band performance. It is directed by Shane Drake who also directed the videos for "Pressure" and "Emergency". It stars Amy Paffrath as the bully.

The music video starts out with the band playing the song with an assortment of "RIOT!"s (a reference to the album's name) in the background. It switches from the band playing to a high school, where a girl in a blue dress and heavy makeup walks in. The girl pushes the school cheerleaders aside as she walks into the hallway. She cuts off another girl's braid with scissors, grinning at the horrified girl while showing it to her. Later, as she is walking down the hall, a boy comes out of the nurse's office with his arm in a sling. She proceeds to push him into the wall, further injuring him. The band plays more, and the girl walks up on a girl and a boy together, obviously in love. She pushes the girl's face out of the way, and passionately kisses the boy, then leaves, grinning smugly. It switches again to the band playing, then the band comes out of a classroom together. Hayley Williams and the girl confront each other in the hall. Hayley reaches into the girl's bra and pulls out "false" pads, then uses a towel and wipes the girl's makeup off, exposing her for what she is. The video ends as the band finishes the song; and they walk away as the girl breaks down, crying.

FBR+ also released an alternate cut of the video that removes the high school clips and features only performance segments.

Concept and blasphemy post

The origin of the song is ambiguous and Williams has given conflicting explanations. The Fueled by Ramen website reports that Williams wrote the song based on feedback the band received after a question she posted on their LiveJournal asking what people were ashamed of. However on the band's LiveJournal, Williams claims the song was written about a past experience involving a male friend who she felt was being manipulated by a girl, and later on when Williams and her friend began to date, she penned the lyrics to "finally explain my side of the story and feel freed of it all". Later, Williams addressed the lyrics in the chorus:

" But God does it feel so good
'Cause I got him where I want him now
And if you could then you know you would
'Cause God it just feels so "

It just feels so good

Williams felt that some might find the use of God "casually. in vain, to be blunt" as blasphemy, and as a Christian, she doesn't want "to be held responsible for causing a lot of people to use my God's name in vain." She posted an explanation and apology on the band's LiveJournal.

The phrase "Misery Business" was first heard on a Stephen King adaptation psycho-thriller film *Misery* (1990).

Track listings

A CD single and two 7" vinyls were released in the UK on 18 June. The CD single features a brand new song, "Stop This Song (Love Sick Melody)", and the two vinyls feature two covers: an electronic remix of "My Hero" by the Foo Fighters, and "Sunday Bloody Sunday" by U2.

In popular culture

In various media

- The song was used in professional StarCraft's Shinhan Bank *Pro League*.
- The song was featured in an episode of the British television soap opera *Hollyoaks* in March 2008 ("Born for This" was also used in another episode in September 2008, and then later "Hallelujah" in October 2008).
- The song is a playable track in the games *Guitar Hero World Tour*, in which Hayley Williams is also a playable character, as well as *Rock Band 3*.
- The song is featured in the 2008 video game, *Saints Row 2*.
- The song is featured on the soundtrack of video game *NHL 08*.
- It is used in a season 7 episode of *Degrassi: The Next Generation*, and included in the *Music from Degrassi: The Next Generation* soundtrack.

Covers

- Metalcore band Sea of Treachery has covered "Misery Business". Hayley Williams was noted for praising their cover of the song.
- Aaron Marsh of Copeland did a live cover. Hayley Williams, was noted praising the cover on Twitter.

Source (edited): "http://en.wikipedia.org/wiki/Misery_Business"

Playing God (song)

"**Playing God**" is a song by American rock band Paramore. It was released on November 15, 2010 as the fifth and last single from the band's third studio album, *Brand New Eyes*. It was written by Hayley Williams, Josh Farro, and Taylor York. It also was the last song that consisted of Josh Farro and Zac Farro. After 7 months of release this song, Paramore will release this June 7th their new single "Monster".

Release

In October, 2010, it was announced "Playing God" would be Paramore's next single on the Alter the Press! website, to be released on November 15, 2010. Lead singer Hayley Williams said on her Twitter: "Miss Anne will be making her final appearance in our new video for "Playing God"… She was the best car. She'll live in our hearts 4ever".

Writing and composition

The song was written by Hayley Williams, Josh Farro and Taylor York. Hayley said she wrote the song at a time when she felt "very angry". Williams also said the song is about people who judge issues concerning faith.

When asked about the development of music during an interview on each track, Hayley said:

"The five of us met at the home of Josh and Zac and sat in the living room with two guitars and [the] bass of Jeremy. Josh and Taylor began playing guitar lines. Of course, we did. I had all sorts of letters on my old Sidekick and used that song was a completely different kind of music in my head. I had it all quickly and with a rude sound. I changed the melody a little and added a few things since Josh created the melody for the chorus. I'm screaming at people who think themselves right, with my own band mates and all that ever made me feel not good enough. But the tone of the music is completely different. It's pretty quiet and fun. When we arrived at the studio, the song still needed a bridge. So I sat at a piano and composed. It's one of my favorite places on the album - I love the call and response that I and Josh did. I feel this is one of those who've been waiting to write for a long time.

—Hayley Williams

Reception

James Montgomery of MTV praised the video, noting: "Paramore are coming home, looking back, wrapping things ... It's a story that began with the band's future in serious doubt and ends with them stronger, happier and better than ever." He also stated; "So if "God" really is the end of the BNE line, well, then it's a fitting farewell. It is time for the band to turn the page, move on." His conclusion was that the video "was a bit of professionalism and fun, and I can not wait to see where they go from here." Emma Gaedeke *Billboard* magazine said: "'Playing God' plays off the same momentum that the video for 'Ignorance' did, as Williams is seen poisoning, detaining and interrogating her male bandmates with a magnifying glass in a dark basement ... While the video is an accurate representation of the ill-harbored feelings that the band once shared, there is no doubt that Paramore has since recovered. By the end of the video, Williams has untied the guys just enough so they can still rock out together, suggesting that while she may not be forgetting the past, she's definitely forgiving."

Music video

The music video to promote the single was filmed on November 2, 2010 and was directed by Brandon Chesbro, who directed the band's previous videos, "The Only Exception" and "Careful". During the video's recording, Brandon posted several comments on his Twitter account, giving the news that the video was recorded during the day, and also revealing the first image from the filming of the video, depicting Hayley as what appears to be a housewife, with a pink hair color. The video was released on November 16. "Playing God" was Paramore's last video with guitarist Josh Farro and drummer Zac Farro in the band.

Plot

The video was filmed entirely in the home of Williams in Franklin, Tennessee. The video begins with Hayley getting out of her car and entering the house. She then enters into a basement where there are four men (Josh, Taylor, Jeremy and Zac) seated and fastened with rope, and a single light bulb hanging over their heads. During the video, Hayley sits at a table with friends, where she starts to remember the moment in which she "poisoned" the men who are now in the basement. The video also shows Hayley as a "bad girl", which many Paramore fans found surprising and amusing. Hayley's friends shown in the video are also personal friends of the band in real life; seen on screen are the girlfriend of Jeremy Davis; Kathryn Camsey, ex-member Hunter Lamb, Brandon Chesbro's wife and new member of the band on tour, Jon Howard. The video is supposed to be a sequel to Ignorance, as she is getting revenge on her band mates for doing the exact same thing to her not too long ago.

Source (edited): "http://en.wikipedia.org/wiki/Playing_God_(song)"

Pressure (Paramore song)

"**Pressure**" is a song by American rock band Paramore. It was released on June 31, 2005 as the first single from their debut album, *All We Know Is Falling*. It failed to chart the *Billboard* Hot 100, however, it managed to peak at #62 on the *Billboard* Hot Digital Songs chart. It was released on April 22, 2006 in the United Kingdom.

Music video

A music video directed by Shane Drake was released for the track in 2005. The video opens with the band playing in an abandoned warehouse. It cuts to an arrival of a man ready for work at a fast food restaurant, but he was late. A girl wants to eat a piece of chocolate and choose her own outfit, but her manager refuses to let her. The man wants to do the work, but then quits his job to see his girlfriend. He arrives, but she was busy preparing for a photo shoot. To win his girlfriend back, he activates the pressure gauges and sets off the sprinklers under the playing band. Zac Farro, Jeremy Davis, Josh Farro, and Hayley Williams then get all wet in the water. The video closes with the couple escaping and the band staying in the water.

Other appearances

- This song was later re-released on the iTunes Deluxe Edition of *Riot!* as a bonus track.
- The song was featured as a track on the console version of *The Sims 2* if you interact with a radio or stereo. As per usual for the series, the song was re-recorded with the lyrics in Simlish.

Covers

- New Found Glory has covered "Pressure" on live version.

Source (edited): "http://en.wikipedia.org/wiki/Pressure_(Paramore_song)"

That's What You Get

"**That's What You Get**" is a single by rock band Paramore. This is the second Australian single, third U.S. single and the fourth UK single from *Riot!*. The single has been confirmed by MTV and Fueled by Ramen. The song was released on radio on March 22 in Australia and on March 24 in the U.S.

In the United States, the song was released on May 5 as a download and physically on May 12. The song is featured in the video game *Rock Band 2*.

The song was certified Gold in the United States on December 12, 2008, selling over 500,000 copies.

Music video

The music video, directed by Marcos Siega, was shot in Nashville, Tennessee, on March 2 and March 3, 2008. MTV2 released the official music video on March 24, 2008. The music video shows the band playing in a living room with clips of a relationship of two lovers (Aaron Holmes of Death in the Park and Jenna Galing, both from Richmond VA) and a small gathering of the band's friends and family. The friends and family are having a good time taking pictures, talking, and listening to music. The two lovers seem to be very much in love with each other. One of the lovers seems to be connected to one of the band members. The two soon go to the gathering where the boy meets someone (maybe an ex-girlfriend) and starts to flirt with her. As the boy continues to spend more time with the other girl, his girlfriend sits on a near couch watching them. As soon as they start holding hands, the girlfriend leaves and starts crying. The end shows the two lovers taking a picture of themselves kissing on a cell phone (before they separated) and all the people rushing out the living room, knocking over the couch and leaving a record spinning.

Background

The music video was shot just over a week after Paramore cancelled their European tour to work on "personal issues", amidst media speculation of the band breaking up. Hayley Williams (lead vocals/keyboard) explained that, given the fragile state of the band, they all thought it best if they kept the shoot low-key, surrounding themselves with their friends and family, keeping it simple.

Hayley added "We had tons of friends there, and it really just felt like a hangout session. And Marcos was so cool about it. He said, 'Bring your friends.' We shot it in some of our friends' houses, and it just felt so real ... and I think it's the first time in a video you're gonna get to see who we really are."

Source (edited): "http://en.wikipedia.org/wiki/That%27s_What_You_Get"

The Only Exception

"**The Only Exception**" is a song by the American rock band Paramore. It was released by Fueled by Ramen in February 2010 as the third single from the band's 2009 studio album *Brand New Eyes*. The song was written by Paramore band members Hayley Williams, Josh Farro and Taylor York; Paramore is also credited as being co-producers to the song. The song was generally well received by music critics; praise of the song was mainly about Williams' vocal performance. Music critics reviewing the song noted that "The Only Exception" was a different musical theme for the band.

"The Only Exception" has been the most successful single from *Brand New Eyes*, and the most successful Paramore single thus far, having topped the United Kingdom Rock Chart and peaked at #13 and #17 in New Zealand and Australia respectively. The single continues to move up on the charts in the *Billboard* Hot 100, where it is the band's third top forty hit to date. A music video for the song, directed by Brandon Chesbro, was released on February 17, 2010, via the band's official website. The song received a Grammy nomination for Best Pop Performance by a Duo or Group with Vocals.

Background

"The Only Exception" was released as the third single from the band's 2009 studio album *Brand New Eyes* in February 2010. It was noticed by music critics that, Paramore, who usually write and record darker material, mainly of the alternative genre, had, musically, gone in a different direction with "The Only Exception". *Rolling Stone* described the song as "a subtle, Radiohead-esque ballad." The song's lyrics pertain to the protagonist not believing that love exists and trying to live without it, mainly to avoid rejection, but eventually realizing that it does exist, describing the person as being their "only exception". Many fans believe that the song was written as an ode to Chad Gilbert from New Found Glory. Incidentally, Wiliams has declined to comment directly on the issue, merely saying, "Read a couple blogs, and you'll figure it out."

Other themes include trying to pursue a relationship, as well as trying to make a relationship last, which can be seen in the lyrics, "In the morning, when you wake up/Leave me with some kind of proof it's not a dream". According to the sheet music published on Musicnotes.com by Alfred Music Publishing, the single is written in the time signature of 6/8 time. The song is played in the key of B major and is sung in the vocal range of F#3 to D#5. "The Only Exception" has a moderately slow tempo of forty eight beats per minute.

Critical reception

"The Only Exception" received generally positive reviews from contemporary music critics. Williams' vocal performance was mainly praised by music critics. Mikael Wood, a writer for *Spin* felt that "The Only Exception" was a "surprisingly soulful acoustic number" and compared its musical structure to Coldplay's *Parachutes*-era. Wood commented that the song was an "upgrade" that consisted of "focus and intensity". Leonie Cooper of *NME* noted in his review for *Brand New Eyes* that Paramore were able to "showcase their maturity" with multiple ballad songs, specifying "The Only Exception". Cooper commented that while the song's lyrics seemed to be a "nondescript love song" that does not "quite warrant the abrupt change of pace", he praised Williams' vocals. Cooper further stated,

"[The song] feels like something Katy Perry would dismiss for being too lightweight, with its mechanical, campfire strumming and general uninspiring air. Its saving grace, however, comes with Williams' vocals, which are flawless and sturdy throughout. Even though the song gets soppy, she never does – weakness just ain't in this lady's repertoire, and for that we offer her a hefty high five."

Marc Hirsh of *The Boston Globe* listed "The Only Exception" as the highlight of *Brand New Eyes*, crediting the song as being an "essential". Hirsh said that "The Only Exception" is "probably the best place to start" with the album, describing Williams' vocals as "forging a connection" rather than "simply spitting out her feelings"; he also praised the other band members for locking in at a "sympathetic simmer". Channing Freeman of Sputnikmusic felt that that "The Only Exception" had similarities to "The Boy Who Blocked His Own Shot" by Brand New. Freeman stated that on Paramore's *All We Know Is Falling*, "My Heart" was a "blunt and obvious song" that focused on a "climax to be emotional", but with "The Only Exception", Paramore have "figured out that it doesn't have to finish loud to incite a reaction in the listener". He also noted that the song shows that Williams' lyrics have "definitely improved". Jesse Catalodo of Slant felt that the lyrics to "The Only Exception" may be "irredeemably over-the-top" but its "vocal melodies are the stuff of perfect pop".

Chart performance

It managed to peak at number thirty eight on the *Billboard* component chart for pop songs; the song remained on the chart for only two weeks. However, on the week of June 12, 2010, the song debuted at number ninety on the Billboard Hot 100. It has since peaked at #24, becoming the most successful Paramore single overall outside of airplay (*Misery Business* remains their most-successful airplay single to date), and their third Top 40 hit in the US. The track was more successful internationally, generally peaking within the top twenty on multiple countries' charts. "The Only Exception" debuted at number number thirty-eight on the New Zealand RIANZ singles chart on February 22, 2010. The following week, the song moved up fifteen positions to number twenty-three, with the song currently having peaked at number thirteen on the country's chart. After four weeks on the chart, "The Only Exception" peaked at number two on the United Kingdom's Rock Chart on March 14, 2010, staying at that position for three weeks but moving up to number one on the chart's issue date of April 5, 2010. The song entered the UK Singles Chart at number eighty on March 28, 2010. It has managed to peak at number thirty-one. The track peaked at number forty-seven in Austria on March 28, 2010. The single also debuted as its peak position, number eighty-four, on the Eurochart Hot 100 Singles chart on April 24, 2010. "The Only Exception" debuted at number fifty-nine in Brazilian Hot 100 Airplay chart in June 2010, becoming the group's first single to enter the Brazilian charts, achieving the following months the position at #32.

Music video

Williams in the song's music video. In the scene Williams is shown lying on Valentine-themed cards while singing the song's chorus. The cards shown in the video were fan-made. Chesbro said that the scene was his favorite part of the video to film.

A music video for "The Only Exception" was directed by Brandon Chesbro, who had been working with Paramore for over two years. The song's music video was Chesbro's music video directorial debut. Prior to "The Only Exception" video, Chesbro had been approached to direct music videos for *Brand New Eyes*' two previous singles, but chose not to due to creative opinions. In December 2009, he was asked to direct the music video for "The Only Exception". Although the story board process took a while, the video was filmed in four days. The music video premiered on February 17, 2010, on Paramore's website. Williams confirmed that as part of a Valentine's Day theme, the band selected cards that were sent to them by fans and featured them in the video. In an interview with MTV, Chesbro commented on filming the scene involving Williams lying on Valentine's Day's styled-cards during the music video, saying,
"The band has crazy fans. All those cards are so detailed [...] these kids spent serious time on these cards. That's my favorite shot of the whole video. It was the first thing we shot and I thought that if something falls apart and we only have that one shot, that could be the video all by itself and it'd be perfect."
The music video opens with Williams waking up on a couch next to an unnamed male and writing a note that says "I'm sorry". From there she walks to the next room and hugs an adult, who, based on the lyrics, is presumed to be her father. A conversation ensues with Williams showing him a photo of someone presumed to be her mother. The video continues with Williams in her room staring into the mirror, singing about how love doesn't exist. She then moves through a costume closet and into a restaurant set, where a rotating cast of men pose as her date. She then moves into the next room, where there's a wedding — everyone is wearing white, but Williams comes dressed in black; she flees the scene when the bride enters. During the chorus of the song, the clip cuts to the scenes where Williams sings "Darling, you are the only exception" while lying down on a giant pile of Valentine-themed cards. Throughout the video, clips of Williams singing with the rest of the members of Paramore in a dim-lighted background are shown, such as Williams sitting down singing into a microphone, and the other members playing instruments. In the video's final moments, Williams spots the same male she woke up to at the beginning of the video in the crowd at a rock show. After fantasizing of the two being together, she then makes her way back through the various rooms to the original set in the beginning of the video. When Williams sings "And I'm, on my way to believing", she returns to the couch where the male is still asleep, and hides the note she wrote in her pocket as she lies back down next to him.

The music video for "The Only Exception" was generally well received by music critics. Kyle Anderson, a writer for MTV, commented that the music video is "by far the most visually interesting and complex clip the group has ever produced." Anderson further stated that "despite the complexity of the video, the whole process was remarkably efficient". She remarked that based on the video's outcome that it was "a little bit surprising" to know that it was directed by a first-time director. Mike Sheffield of *Spin* viewed the music video as a "love story" and described it as being "Valentine's Day + epic Emo balladry = Paramore's brand new video for 'The Only Exception'". Chesbro said that he was happy with the final product of the music video and that directing the video made him become more interested in directing videos, saying, "I'd really like to do more videos now [...] This video turned out so perfect that I'm worried nothing else will turn out as good. But if this is my only video, I was super-proud to be a part of it."

Live performances

The track has been performed by Paramore on many occasions. The band's first performance of the song was on November 1, 2009 in Nashville. Paramore performed a live version of "The Only Exception" for *The Ellen Degeneres Show*.

The band performed the chorus and outro of the song on the *2010 MTV Video Music Awards* on September 12, 2010.

The Only Exception EP is Paramore's third extended play (EP), released exclusively to the iTunes Store on September 28, 2010.

Personnel

The following personnel contributed to "The Only Exception":

See also

- List of number-one rock hits of 2010 (UK)
- List of number-one rock hits of 2011 (UK)

In popular culture

Live performances

- Paramore performed a live version of "The Only Exception" for *The Ellen Degeneres Show*.
- The band performed the chorus and outro of the song on the *2010 MTV Video Music Awards* on September 12, 2010.
- Paramore performed "The Only Exception" in VH1 Divas 2010 with the song Misery Business, Decode and My Hero
- The band performed "The Only Exception" in in Madison Square Garden with the song Misery Business and Brick by Boring Brick

Other appearances

- The music video appears in Paramore's Videos. All of Them. Ever.
- The song appears in 2011 Grammy Nominees by the Nominees in 53rd Grammy Awards.

Covers

- Sam Tsui and Kurt Schneider did a acoustic cover.
- April Chase did a cover, the Directed an shot is Marco Bercasio
- Rachel G. Fox did a acoustic cover

Glee cover

The song was performed in the Britney Spears-themed episode "Britney/Brittany" of the US television series *Glee*, which aired September 28, 2010. Lea Michele, in character as Rachel Berry, sang the song at the end of the episode as an apology to her boyfriend Finn Hudson, played by Cory Monteith. The performance was praised by most critics, with *Rolling Stone*'s Erica Futterman calling it "gorgeous and tender" and *Entertainment Weekly*'s Tim Stack praising it as the episode's "nice, emotional capper". Hayley Williams complimented Michele's vocals on the rendition through her Twitter account. The cover was released as a single and charted at number twenty-two in both Canada and Ireland, twenty-six in the US, and sixty in Australia, with sales of 89,000 copies in the US according to Nielsen SoundScan.

References

Source (edited): "http://en.wikipedia.org/wiki/The_Only_Exception"